GOD LOVES THE FREAKS

Stephen Weese

Publisher: Lulu.com
Cover: Stephen Weese
Back Cover: Rebecca Suman
Edited by: Stephen Weese and Ann Parkinson

ISBN: 978-1-4303-0365-7

**For all my friends at Fans for Christ,
this one's for you.**

48,148

Acknowledgements

There are a number of varied and wondrous people that have helped make this book a reality. This is the part where I talk about them and flatter them unashamedly so they can say they have their names in a book.

First of all, my dear friend Ann Parkinson, who not only offered moral support but editing as well. May she be famous and cool forever.

All my friends at Fans for Christ, you had this book dedicated to you so don't say I've never done anything for ya. But you also helped with ideas and other contributions for this book.

Becky Suman drew me a very nice design which is used on the back cover of this book. Also, Tif, Sparkles, Coolest Punk Chick ever, however you want to be called, thanks for your last minute help with things.

Thanks to my old friend Zach van der Meer (look I got your name right!) for support and great conversations about what this book means. Thanks to Vic Mignogna and Brandy Ledford for the interviews and letting me quote them in the book.

David Dellman, who is the director of Gothic Christianity, thanks for the marvelous introduction. I hope people don't skip to the first chapter (like I usually do) and actually read it. Because, hey, it's good.

Thanks to the Haven X Obscurum folks for letting me get my preview edition out to the Christian Goth community. Hey now you'll have an edited book to read! There you go, Lectra and Kryss.

Kris Trader gave me a nice cover design for the preview edition (with blood!) so thanks for that. Donna Sheehy, thanks for your support of me and my book. I guess Mike can have some credit too, Donna.

My friend Heather, who helped me make it through maybe the worst time in my life, there's not much else I can say but thanks again. To my Lost Kitty – I hope you get to read this book and it inspires you to great things.

Thanks to Jason Gore and Jeff Ramsey, the guys at the brand new sparkly church, Visio Dei. Though you chose to meet at

10 in the morning, I still love you guys. Thanks for making worship service and church community fresh and real.

Thanks to Chris Lutyk for being a great mentor through all my rough years learning about being a Christian. His family is great too – Nora, Chip, Anthony, Daniel, Tessa, Sasha… God bless you guys.

Thanks to Mom and Dad for being my mom and dad. Of course, thanks be to God for all he has done. Thanks for making me a freak Lord, I wouldn't have it any other way.

-- Stephen Weese
November, 2006

Introduction

"Come, ye blessed of my Father, inherit the kingdom prepared for you from the foundation of the world: For I was an hungered, and ye gave me meat: I was thirsty, and ye gave me drink: I was a stranger, and ye took me in: Naked, and ye clothed me: I was sick, and ye visited me: I was in prison, and ye came unto me. Then shall the righteous answer him, saying, Lord, when saw we thee hungered and fed thee? Or thirsty, and gave thee drink? When saw we thee a stranger, and took thee in? Or naked, and clothed thee? Or when saw we thee sick, or in prison, and came unto thee? And the King shall answer and say unto them, Verily I say unto you, Inasmuch as ye have done it unto one of the least of these my brethren, ye have done it unto me,"

– The Words of Jesus in Matthew 25: 34 – 40

As the passage referenced above suggests, to some extent, we will be judged by how we treat others, and not just those we find attractive or those that are the most like us, but those distinctly not like us. Jesus was a lover of the outcast, the downtrodden, and the rejected, and He expects those who wish to be identified with His name to follow His example.

Reaching out to others is a natural outcome of a life lived in God, but sometimes fear gets in the way.

1st John 4: 18 – 19 says, "There is no fear in love; but perfect love casteth out fear: because fear hath torment. He that feareth is not made perfect in love. We love him, because he first loved us." This passage has more to say but I will hold that thought until the end of this introduction.

Fear is a natural response to the unfamiliar. But, where love is present, that natural response is overcome. This book will help you overcome fear and misunderstanding, it will help you appreciate the rich diversity of people that God has created.

Sometimes it is not fear that inhibits the believers' expression of love but familiarity and personal comfort. The indwelling Holy Spirit will naturally urge all believers to move beyond their personal comfort zone in an effort to reach someone that does not know of God's love. Even the Apostles tended to cling to that which was familiar or comfortable.

"Despite Jesus' orders to engage in the gentile mission (Acts 1:8), the apostles stayed in Jerusalem and remained there as late as Acts 15:2. It is ultimately the bicultural minority within the Jerusalem church (Acts 6:1 – 8: 40) that holds the promise for the future." – Craig Keener, the IVP Bible Background Commentary, p. 339.

Later, as Paul brought many of various gentile nations into Christ, a controversy arose within the church. It was known as the Judaizing heresy because, in essence, the Jewish Christians wanted to force Gentile Christian to abandon their culture and adapt to Jewish Christian culture.

Time and time again in the Book of Acts, and indeed throughout history, when the church is willing to reach out to and embrace those of difference, the church grows and the people are filled with God's love and with His Spirit. But, when the church refuses to reach out, love and embrace, it stagnates like a tree that is strangled by its own roots.

Historically and Biblically, it is the "bicultural" people, as Craig Keener calls them, that God uses in astounding ways.

In the 1960's evangelicals said the Hippies couldn't be reached, that they were lost in drugs and debauchery. When God touched the Hippie movement, the Jesus People were born, and in 1974, they shared the love of Christ with me and I was born again. In the 1970's evangelicals said there could never be revival among the Catholics and yet God poured His Spirit out on Catholicism ushering in a revival that continues to this day. And now, after the start of the new millennium, they say freaks are unreachable. But God is calling all people unto Himself, of every tribe and nation.

This book will help you move past your comfort zone to obedience, and from obedience to love.

The love of the believer is measured in the practical ways it finds expression especially toward those unlike the believer. I mentioned earlier that I would get back to the text in 1st John. The rest of the test says this. "If a man says, I love God, and hateth his brother, he is a liar: for he that loveth not his brother whom he hath seen, how can he love God whom he hath not seen? And this commandment have we from him, That he who loveth God love his brother also," 1st John 4: 20 – 21.

Look around, chances are your brother or sister is a freak. God Loves the Freaks. What about you?

- David Dellman, November 2006

Contents

Chapter 1

Who are the Freaks?

Your first reaction to this book might be similar to your first reaction to someone you consider a freak. You do a double take, stop and look again. Maybe you quickly turn and walk away. Freaks provoke a reaction, either way. Maybe you feel like you are a freak yourself and that is why you are reading this. In that case, you might feel excited about reading this text. Though we all may feel a bit freakish at times, we all do not consider ourselves freaks. So, what is a freak?

A quick trip to dictionary.com reveals this definition:

Freak n. 1: a person or animal that is markedly unusual or deformed

This definition will serve well for us. Some people are markedly unusual, so different that society has a reaction to them. This reaction is usually of the negative sort. For many of us, this is just a fact of life. We are used to things being this way. We look the other way or avoid others that are noticeably different than us.

As Christians, should we join society in isolating these freaks, leaving them out in the cold? You would probably say, "No, of course not, we should reach out to them." Yet, what happens is not only does Christianity not accept those who look, feel, or act differently than the social norm, but they try to change them and make them fit into the cultural mold. This mold says what a good Christian should look like, talk like, dress like, and generally act like. What it means to these different, creative people, those that might be considered freaks, is that they have to give up their unique differences that God gave them.

Don't get me wrong; sin is sin, and Christians are commanded to stay away from it. However, being different or unusual generally is not sinful. Some people see life from a different perspective, have unique experiences that are truly their own. As a result they may talk about unusual topics, or dress differently, even creatively. They may be part of a subculture that shares their interests; like a hippie, or a skater, or a goth. Of course some things about these subcultures may conflict with Christianity, but not all things. One could be part of these subcultures and still be a Christian. In fact, a person like this would be better equipped to reach out to others in that culture.

Think about this: the world is full of many cultures. Nations all over the world have Christians who have diverse backgrounds. Depending on where a person grows up, their social class, sex, and parentage may all directly influence the culture they have. People in Africa, Asia and the Middle East all have different styles of dress, different foods they like, different interests, and different music. God wanted people from many nations to be part of his Kingdom. He is the author of diversity. Why should everyone in a church look the same, talk the same, and have the same interests? Shouldn't *we* desire to see God's Kingdom reflecting *his* desire?

Who are these freaks?

If you went to high school in the United States, then you probably have a good idea of how people form into social groups. You also have seen how certain groups have a higher status than others. Most of us will be able to think of how the Cheerleaders and the Jocks were near the top. People like the Chess Club and the nerds who read comics were closer to the bottom. The people at the bottom were often ridiculed, isolated, and worse. In their isolation, they sought each other's company. A few of them had crazy colored hair or wore all black all the time. Just because they were different, or because they didn't fit someone's definition of cool, they were pushed to the fringes of the social group.

Depending on where you live, different groups can be isolated. Different kinds of people can feel alone. So what people do we mean by freaks? Anyone isolated from society for their differences. Nerds, geeks, gamers, Goths, hippies, punks, skaters, poets, artists, and musicians are a few. People with mental illnesses or physical deformities also fit this description. Some people are just so plain different they are their own subculture; they do things their own way. In any case, what makes these people freaks is that they are different from the mainstream, and they are isolated because of it.

Freaks and Geeks

In my experience, there are two main things that seem to isolate these people from others: their style of dress and their interests. What happens to these people when they encounter Christians is that they face stereotypes and also false information about their interests. A stereotype of people that listen to heavy metal music is that they worship Satan, yet there are many Christian heavy metal bands. People also are under the false notion that if you read Harry Potter or other fantasy novels that mention "magic" you are involved in the occult. However, the truth is that these are works of fiction and not based on reality. They simply are about a different world or reality where magic exists as a natural force. Sane people realize these are works of fiction and don't run around with self-made magic wands trying to cast spells. They just enjoy the stories.

People might like going to renaissance faires and dressing up in medieval costumes, yet some Christians might assume they are pagans or involved in some kind of cult. This is because they simply don't know about the actual culture and interests of certain types of people. How many of you have heard that the game Dungeons and Dragons (D&D) is evil? I personally have run into this issue many times, and mostly from people who have never seen one single rulebook of the actual game. They think people do strange things with strange occult ceremonies while playing this game. What really happens is we sit around, drink soda and eat snacks, make jokes and roll dice to play the game. This really isn't much different than your average Monopoly session. (See the Appendix on D&D and fantasy for more details on Dungeons and Dragons.) Many geeks and nerds play D&D and collect comic books. We like to use our imagination and create stories. Not everyone has to like these kind of games, but judging them as "evil" without knowing anything firsthand about them is just wrong.

Cultural Differences

If someone came to church from an African country and wore traditional African clothes, we would most likely accept their style of dress. Yet, if a punk from our own country came to church with a big pink Mohawk, we would likely have a different reaction. Why are we more accepting of differences that are international than differences inside our culture? Is there anything sinful about a huge pink Mohawk? Inside the punk culture, a Mohawk is perfectly normal. However, most Christian churches would probably try to convince this person to change. We would not ask the African to change, but we would ask the punk. Think about that. There is a notion that all Americans should fit into the mold of what I would call "American Christianity." If you are an American and you are Christian, then you must dress a certain way. However, God made us all different and we should accept those differences whether they are international or local.

Somehow we have taken Christianity and added our own culture to it. We have decided that to be a Christian you must not only believe in Jesus as your savior, and the Bible, but you must also wear certain clothes, talk a certain way, only listen to certain music, and do many other things that are cultural but not Christian in origin. In this book we will see the problems that go along with making Christianity more than it should be.

Thinking outside the box

I believe that a common problem many Christians have is assuming stereotypes about a certain culture. We see someone dressing a certain way, and we automatically assume many things about them, instead of looking at them as an individual. For example, one time I was in a bookstore to meet with my pastor. I was dressed as I often do, all in black, with combat boots and spikes. A man came up to me and asked, "Excuse me, but what cult do you belong to?" Imagine his surprise when I told him I was a Christian, and I was there to meet my pastor for lunch! Everyone has a different reason for doing what they do, and being who they are.

A common response I will hear is that people act or dress differently out of immaturity. The reasoning goes is that these freaks want to stand out either to frighten people or to get attention for others. So, it is said that if these people were really mature they would stop being this way and act and dress like everyone else. Besides that fact that this would make for a very *boring* world to live in, it also is an incorrect assumption. Some people simply feel comfortable with the clothes they wear, or their style. They wear it because, shockingly, they *like* it. It is a beautiful thing that we have freedom to wear what we like, to express ourselves. Instead of assuming bad things about those who are different, we could perhaps wonder what their story is. We could learn from their unique perspective on life.

Freaks for a reason

Everyone has their own social groups that they join; it is natural. We tend to spend time with others who share our interests and culture. For the freaks of the world, they group together for this reason and more; they bond over their isolation. Society is harder on those who don't fit into the mainstream. People treat freaks worse than others. Chances are when you meet someone like this, they have been wounded by society, made to feel an outcast. Some may even believe that there is something *wrong* with them because they like different things than others, so they hide inside their outcast social groups. They may tend to be angry, sorrowful, or more emotional than most people. Freaks come together over their shared pain and isolation.

I am a big sci-fi and fantasy nerd. A few times a year, I get to go to a convention for sci-fi and fantasy. I am surrounded by people wearing Storm Trooper outfits, carrying swords, and wearing T-shirts with gaming slogans on them. I know most of the people there could tell me how fast the Millennium Falcon can fly, the names of all the Hobbits from Lord of the Rings, and how Warp Drive technology works. When I am at these conventions I think, "*These* are my people!" They know how it feels to be made fun of for not knowing who won the football game because they were watching Star Trek all night. I love these people, largely because they are like me. Because I love them, I want them to know God. Let me ask you, how many churches or groups think to evangelize at a sci-fi convention? The freaks will stay isolated if no one reaches out to them.

Treating Freaks Right

What all this really comes down to is that these freaks are neglected and shunned by not only mainstream society, but also Christianity. The problem for Christians is twofold: First, they do not reach out to these people. Second, they do not accept different or weird people who are Christians. Instead they try to change them, make them into traditional American Christian culture.

When it comes to evangelism, it may be a challenge for traditional Christians to witness to subcultures. We tend to speak our own language, which I often refer to as "Christianese" that is confusing to others outside of our realm. We say things like "I felt in my Spirit," or "I interceded about this," or perhaps "I was convicted about something." A non-Christian hearing the last one might think you were arrested and found guilty! We should speak in plain language, at least outside of the church. So, instead of the phrases above we could say things like, "I felt God saying to me," or "I spent time in prayer about this," or "I felt in my heart I was doing something wrong." Regardless, Christians should make an effort to reach out to these people. After all, it wasn't the well-dressed or the glorious that Jesus reached out to in the Bible. If we speak in a way that can be understood, our message will be clearer.

Dealing with the second problem may be harder, where we try to change believers into a mold. American Christian culture has a certain set of unwritten rules on how you should live. Including what words you can use, how you dress, how you spend your free time, even perhaps what kind of car you drive. Somehow we have made trivial things like this an important part of the Christian life. We also have a class system of Christians in many churches. If you dress and talk and act the recommended way, you are on the first tier. You can then be considered for leadership in the church, and have people look up to you. But if you don't fit in, don't pray every day when you get up, don't dress according to the rules, or stand out in some way, you belong to the second class. You aren't considered a candidate for leadership. Others in the church will try to "convert" you to be part of the elite, the "better" Christians. They may even feel sorry for you, or make you into a project so you will be more like them.

Have you seen this happening? It happens everywhere. People that God made different, creative, and unique are being compressed into a cookie cutter mold of Christianity. Yet when this happens, God's will, I suggest to you, is not done. Instead we deprive the church, and that person, of a special uniqueness that God himself gave to them. In the pages ahead, we will take a look at God's view on different kinds of people. We will look at the effects of culture on Christianity. The idea is to find out what truly is important in our lives, and what things are not. If we rid ourselves of these extra rules that squash everyone into the same mold, we will begin to represent the diversity that God intended for us. If you still think that these freaks need to be changed, re-molded into a "regular person" read on and examine these insights into the people who many would label freaks.

Chapter 2

Why are people different?

There are so many factors that make people unique in many respects. In today's society, we generally are exposed to movies, media, and information from countries all over the world. We see different styles of dress, different family structures, and different social values. Yet, for some reason, while we are aware of all these differences, when we live our every day lives, most of us are not as tolerant of these differences as we should be. We can watch for instance, *The Last Samurai* with Tom Cruise, about an American in 1800's Japan, yet leave the theater and go right back to our traditional ideas of what people should be like. Even though someone watching this movie sees a culture with radically different ideas of honor and how people should live, it is only a momentary entertainment. Somehow all the differences in the world bounce right off of us. It is almost as if only our little world is real, only America is real and the rest of the world is a dream, or a novel. Yet there are many cultures out there that have different ideas on how to eat a meal, how to greet others, and what actions convey respect and disrespect. There are many reasons people are different, and many cultures and ideas of how to live life. It is incorrect to assume that our way of doing things is always the best way. These cultural differences are, for the most part, not bad or good, simply different.

Geography

Geography is a big reason why people are different. Where you grow up determines so much about you. Remember back to the Tower of Babel in Genesis. God scattered all the people around the earth and gave them different languages. Each nation has its own national heritage. As I mentioned before, if you ran into a cultural African in your church, and they still wore traditional African dress, you would probably be more accepting of them than someone with a mohawk.

Imagine a church with people from nations all over the world. There would be Africans, Japanese, French, Swedes, Australians, Icelanders, Filipinos, and Brazilians (to name a few) all together at a worship service. They all might dress differently, and speak different languages, but they would all be worshipping the one true God. We would probably take this vision as a beautiful manifestation of God's grace to the whole world. It might even bring a tear to our eye if we really stopped to depict it clearly in our minds.

Now, imagine the same thing, except a church full of the freaks. You see nerds, hippies, Goths, punks, skaters, medieval re-enactors, and artists all worshipping together. Would you have the same reaction? Or would you feel awkward and wish they all would learn to dress right and like the right music and entertainment?

If we really thought about it, however, the cultural differences in the first church would be huge. They would have different ideas on marriage, material possessions, how to talk, what is courteous, how you dressed, and even how to decorate your house!

Even inside the United States, geography affects cultural rules. Someone from New York City would have a different background than someone from Alabama. Even people from New York State outside of the city are very different culturally. We have areas with different levels and types of spirituality. We have areas that are hard, and you have to be tough and look out for yourself, while others are more friendly and supportive. Imagine someone from a tough area; they may seem unfriendly to others, but they are really doing what they have learned they need to do to survive.

There is often a culture shock when someone moves from one region of the United States to another. Imagine moving from the West Coast to the Midwest. Or moving from North Dakota to Miami, Florida. America is very diverse in itself. Just because we are used to one region or area, does not make our culture the "right" one. Christianity in these different areas can be affected by the culture. In the Bible Belt of the south, the impact on the culture is large. There are just some things you don't "do" there, yet they might be perfectly acceptable in other regions.

Geographic differences on culture are very apparent in the Bible. The Israelites often encountered cultures that considered human sacrifice acceptable. (Not that it is a correct thing to do, it merely illustrates a difference.) Paul, when he speaks to the Greeks in the Areopagus addresses the Greeks on their own cultural terms, not in the Hebrew terms that he would be steeped in growing up as a Pharisee. (Acts 17) God surprised everyone when he said that salvation was for everyone, both Jews and the Gentiles. The Jews were shocked and amazed that God wanted to reach out and offer salvation to the "Gentiles", people of other races.

The early Christians themselves were not innocent of allowing culture to influence their beliefs. In Acts 15, we read about how many of the Jewish believers were requiring that new Gentile Christians obey all of the Old Testament laws. They even were requiring *adult* males to be circumcised! Culture has a powerful impact upon us all, and it is not an easy thing to let go. However, the apostles got together and addressed this issue. They determined that there were only a few laws from the Old Testament that applied to the new believers. James got up and spoke:

> It is my judgment, therefore, that we should not
> make it difficult for the Gentiles who are turning to
> God. Instead we should write to them, telling them
> to abstain from food polluted by idols, from sexual
> immorality, from the meat of strangled animals and
> from blood. --Acts 15:19-20

We can make it difficult for freaks to become Christians when we require them to change much about themselves and lose their culture. Instead we should focus on the heart, and on faith, and on knowing God. Just like the Jews were making it hard for these Gentiles, we can turn people away from God by making it about too many rules.

Prevailing social philosophy and generation

Different generations of people will grow into adults during different social movements. Some generations have predominant social movements, like the radical movement during the sixties of "free love." Other generations have more of a mix, where there is not a particular movement that dominates. These people will have more of a variety of views on morality and theology.

The differences between generations are so marked that we even identify generations by different names: Baby Boomers, Baby Busters, Generation X, and Generation Y, for example. If you are a parent, you know the difference between you and your children. If not, you can remember how what *you* thought was cool as a teenager your parents had *no clue* about.

Many churches are now offering what are called "contemporary" services. These services usually appeal to the younger churchgoers. Why? The music is new, played with guitars and even drums. It is more like the music that younger generations listened to as they grew up. Many older Christians are used to the traditional hymns and that is what they are comfortable with. Does this mean that either one is wrong? Would we say that the older people should change with the times and like the newer music? Should we tell the teenagers that hymns are what we always have done, and that is what we always will do? It may be obvious that the answers to these questions should be "no." Yet generational gaps still cause divides between people. It seems the older generations are always down on the younger generations for the way they dress, or what music they listen to. Yet, when that older generation was younger the music they listened to and the clothes they wore were radical for the generation before them. This is simply how life goes, through each generation. The younger generations tend to not respect those older than them. Why can't we recognize these patterns and look past them? So many things divide us, when God's plan for his church is unity.

When I was a teenager I had long hair. My grandmother hated my long hair. Every time I would come to visit she would make a big fuss about it and complain about how it looked terrible and that long hair was for girls. Now my grandmother claimed to be a Christian, and she even had a portrait of Jesus up on the wall. One day when I was fed up with her complaining about my hair I finally said, "Well, Grandmother, Jesus had long hair, wasn't it okay for him?" The only thing she could say was, "Yes, but, well… that was different!" Now maybe Jesus didn't really have long hair, but the point is, why was it so important to her that I fit her cultural expectations? We could have focused on good things instead of being divided by petty differences.

Life experience and genetics

Current experts on personality agree that we are a combination of our experiences and our genes. There is some disagreement on the ratio of how much these influence us, yet they are still the two dominant forces that make up our personalities. You may have heard it referred to by the term, "Nature vs. Nurture." Nature would be our genetic predispositions, while "nurture" refers to our upbringing and experiences in life.

On opposite ends of the life experience spectrum, there are two kinds of people. On one end, there are the people who have experienced little suffering and trouble in their lives. Generally, they tend to be less understanding of those in trouble and suffering, because they haven't experienced it for themselves. Some of these people sit back in their easy life, and look down on those who struggle and think that if they only tried harder, they wouldn't have so many troubles. Some Christians who haven't faced much hardship or temptation tend to do this. When other people are struggling with sin, they often answer, "Well, you should just stop," as if it were so easy. The people on the other end of the spectrum have been through much suffering. They have either become bitter from it, or more understanding of the weakness of others.

I have struggled on and off with anxiety throughout my adult life. I was at a particular church that was very strict about many unimportant things. I worried about so many small things, what I said, what I wore, how I looked to others. The anxiety grew and grew. Many days I would lie in my bed with my heart pounding so hard that it would literally shake the bed. Finally, I reached out to one of our pastors for help. I told him I was having trouble with anxiety. His answer was simple, "Well, anxiety is a sin, so you should stop."

All this did was make everything worse. I honestly believed that he must be right, and that I should just be able to stop. Then I began to worry I was sinning because I was anxious and couldn't stop, and what happened? I became even more anxious. Eventually I was able to see a good Christian counselor who talked me through my anxiety issues and had sympathy. The pastor I talked to had no idea about anxiety disorders because he had not experienced them himself. He was able to turn off his anxiety, so, why not everyone else? It is easy to judge when you have not been in a situation, but we should remember that sometimes things are not easy. Jesus knew that his disciples were wanting to stay up and pray with him in the garden, but their flesh was weak.

> Then he returned to his disciples and found them sleeping. "Simon," he said to Peter, "are you asleep? Could you not keep watch for one hour? Watch and pray so that you will not fall into temptation. The spirit is willing, but the body is weak."
> - Mark 14:37-38

They fell asleep in their weakness. We all are weak sometimes. Perhaps we should remember our own weaknesses before judging others. The people on the other end of the spectrum who have suffered much in life realize how weak they are. They know they have made many mistakes. Those who know God are very grateful for his mercy, and humble in their weakness, knowing how much they need him. Sometimes those that have suffered can be envious or angry at those who have not suffered, but they should remember that those who have not suffered simply cannot understand life in the same way.

Our genes also play a significant part in who we are. Studies have shown that a person can inherit traits, like aggressiveness, from parents. We inherit a lot of who we are from our predecessors. Of course, we also inherit the sin nature as part of our fallen flesh. Not everything we inherit is good, yet we all have our different areas of weakness.

There is so much diversity in our physical bodies; height, eye color, skin tone, hair, and facial features make humans a truly diverse race. We have recognized that differences in our physical appearance, our bodies, are normal and that discriminating against those of a different race is immoral. Many of our preferences and things we like are also genetic. Now, if those preferences are sin;

that is one thing. However, if these preferences are just outside of the norm of society, merely *different*, we should accept those unique qualities in people as well. In fact, I will suggest to you that it is just as wrong to isolate and dislike people that have different tastes in clothes, music, food, or perhaps entertainment as it is to be a racist. God made us a beautiful tapestry of color and diversity. We should embrace these differences, rather than try to make everyone conform to the same mold.

Family Influences

When I was a small child, I based my reality on what I saw my family do. The way my mother and father acted toward each other was the normal way that mommies and daddies act. I thought everyone else's parents were just like mine. My parents also had certain rules we had to obey, and a certain way of disciplining us. They showed love in certain ways. My other relatives also shaped how I viewed life.

"Granddad" is what we called my grandfather on my father's side. We used to visit our Granddad and when we saw him and every time he would give us a dollar. He didn't have much to say, he really didn't give us hugs, but he gave us a dollar. I asked my Mom one day why he always gave us a dollar. She said, "That is the only way he knows how to show you he loves you." My father also was not very expressive. It is very hard for him to show emotion or affection. I saw this as what a man should be like: tough, gruff, and strong. Don't say too much and don't put up with much. I knew my Dad loved me, but my impression of what it is to be a man was influenced by him.

Many people's parents tell them things as a child that stay with them. "You never are good enough," they might have said, or "you just can't do anything right." Sometimes they might hear, "Why can't you be like your brother?" Some of these people may feel so inferior that they stop trying to succeed. They are encouraged to fail by the words that were meant to inspire success. A lot of people who are socially different now are that way because as a child, they were not accepted for who they were.

Think about the wonderful feeling of being accepted for who you are. God accepts us and loves us, right where we are today. We don't have to change to be loved. Yet many people have never known this kind of love. When the love from family is withheld based on their performance in school, sports, music, or church, they are not being accepted for who they are. When one feels unloved an unaccepted by society, he will turn away from it and be isolated. Many people who are freaks today, the outcasts, are people who simply were never loved by anyone.

Our parents and relatives shape our views of what we think people should be like. They also shape our view of what we think of ourselves, and what we should be like. Most people spend years and years with their families, and continue to have contact with them as adults. This type of closeness will definitely have a large influence on someone's life. So when you see someone who has a different idea of "how things should be" than you, remember, it may be what they have been taught all their life.

Chapter 3

Jesus was a Freak seeker

For John came neither eating nor drinking, and they say,
'He has a demon.' The Son of Man came eating and drinking, and
they say, 'Here is a glutton and a drunkard, a friend of tax
collectors and "sinners." ' –Matthew 11:18-19

Jesus went out of his way to interact with the members of society
that were outcast. How many times did we hear of him talking to
those that the Pharisees of the day had forbidden contact with?

> When a Samaritan woman came to draw water,
> Jesus said to her, "Will you give me a drink?" (His
> disciples had gone into the town to buy food.)
> The Samaritan woman said to him, "You are a Jew
> and I am a Samaritan woman. How can you ask me
> for a drink?" (For Jews do not associate with
> Samaritans.) – John 4:7-9

Jews did not associate with Samaritans. Christians do not
associate with freaks. What would they think of you in church, if
they saw you out talking with prostitutes? What if they heard you
were out with some Goths? What if someone found out you met
with some people to play Dungeons and Dragons? Jesus cared
about Samaritans; he cared about everyone. As long as they would
listen to him, he would talk to them. Jesus was around these kind
of people so much they called him a friend to tax collectors, a
friend to sinners. That is just what he was, he was their friend. It
didn't matter what they had done, as long as they wanted him as a
friend, he was there. What has happened to the church today that it
does not reach out to these outcasts? Have we forgotten how Jesus
was? Sometimes we Christians can be more like the Pharisees than
we are like Jesus.
     A friend of mine, Vic, is a voice actor for many popular
Japanese animation (anime) shows, and also a Christian who is a

leader in his church. His job is to re-dub the voices for anime into English. One weekend he was invited as a guest for an anime convention at a hotel. The same hotel was also being used for a Christian convention for teens. During the convention, Vic and many others noticed that the Christian teens were often making fun of the anime convention attendees. At anime conventions, many people dress up as their favorite animation character. A lot of these kids were being made fun of for it. Vic went and spoke to one of the leaders of the Christian convention and told him who he was. The leaders decided to let him speak to the teens. Vic told them about anime, and about his job as a voice actor. He also told them that he was a Christian and served in his church. He said to those teens, "You should be out there sharing God with them, getting to know them, talking to them." All they had to do was walk up and say hello. Perhaps they could ask about the costume they were wearing or what anime they liked. When Vic was done, a change happened at that hotel. The teens were talking to the anime kids. Around the hotel you could see teens from both conventions together, talking, and laughing. Straight-laced teens who would never dream of getting dressed in a wild anime costume were walking next to those wearing them. Something wonderful happened: they bonded. They bridged the gap between fear and ignorance with love. The teens shared God with those anime kids that were there, and even made friends with them. What made the difference? Just a change in perspective. Simply saying hello and caring about one of these people that others might consider a freak.

When Jesus reached the spot, he looked up and said to him, "Zacchaeus, come down immediately. I must stay at your house today." So he came down at once and welcomed him gladly.

All the people saw this and began to mutter, "He has gone to be the guest of a 'sinner.' "

But Zacchaeus stood up and said to the Lord, "Look, Lord! Here and now I give half of my possessions to the poor, and if I have cheated anybody out of anything, I will pay back four times the amount." Luke 19:5-8

Look at this example of Jesus. He says to someone that is shunned by society, "I am going to be your guest! I will even come into your house!" Today a wealthy IRS agent might be looked up to, but in the Jewish society tax collectors were looked down upon. This was not without good reason; many of them were indeed crooked and took more than their share of tax money. However, look at the contrast in results as compared to the Pharisees.

> Every day he was teaching at the temple. But the chief priests, the teachers of the law and the leaders among the people were trying to kill him. --Luke 19:47

The "holy" people heard his message every day at the temple. That's where all the holy rollers were to be found, trying to look holy. What was their response? They wanted to kill him. Yet, Zacchaeus' response was much different. All it took was one good man to accept him, talk to him, and be his friend to turn him away from his sin. He didn't have to hear the message over and over, he immediately gave to the poor and repaid his stolen money. Many freaks are like this man. No one has really tried to accept or love them, at least, not from the Christian community. Yet when one person genuinely does reach out, a heart can respond with joy. Zacchaeus probably had heard all the time how he was so terrible from the Pharisees, he wasn't going to listen to them or even be around them. Can you imagine the looks they would give him? The things they would say about him? Yet Jesus talked to him like a friend and came to his house. He was not ashamed to be seen with him. Think about that. Jesus was not ashamed to be seen, in public, with an outcast. Can you say the same?

Who is a sinner?

You may be thinking to yourself, "Well, those people that Jesus talked to were *sinners,* they needed to hear the gospel and repent! I could go up to them and tell them about God, but I couldn't be friends with *sinners.* " What is a sinner then? Clearly, a sinner would be someone who sins. Committing a sin means disobeying God's will. The Bible makes it clear we all have sinned.

> Therefore, just as sin entered the world through one
> man, and death through sin, and in this way death
> came to all men, because all sinned -- Romans 5:12

> There is no difference, for all have sinned and fall
> short of the glory of God, and are justified freely by
> his grace through the redemption that came by
> Christ Jesus. -- Romans 3:22-24

So, in this sense we are all sinners. Now the Bible does sometimes
speak of sinners in a separate sense from those who are saved.
Jesus says in Luke 15 that there will be more rejoicing in heaven
over one sinner who repents than over ninety-nine righteous
persons who do not need to repent.

What makes a sinner separate from the righteous? Apparently the
need to repent. In fact, Jesus' message was very simple, it was to
repent and believe.

> After John was put in prison, Jesus went into
> Galilee, proclaiming the good news of God. "The
> time has come," he said. "The kingdom of God is
> near. Repent and believe the good news!" Mark
> 1:14-15

Why do we repent? What is repentance? The Greek word used in
the Bible for repentance literally means to "change one's mind."
(Strongs #3340) Change one's mind about what? About sinning.
So, we change our minds to no longer follow the ways of sin. We
change our minds to follow God and his spirit.

> So I say, live by the Spirit, and you will not gratify
> the desires of the sinful nature. For the sinful nature
> desires what is contrary to the Spirit, and the Spirit
> what is contrary to the sinful nature. They are in
> conflict with each other, so that you do not do what
> you want. But if you are led by the Spirit, you are
> not under law. Galatians 5:16-18

Our new changed minds, with the Spirit of God in us, can now follow God's spirit. We have a different way of living. Yet the verse above also says you do not do what you want, because of the conflict. We are still conflicted people. Becoming a Christian does not mean you stop sinning. We are still sinners, yet we have changed our minds and now follow a different leader, Jesus, and the Spirit, and the Father.

Jesus goes out of his way to remind the self-righteous that they are still sinners. In John 8, a group of Pharisees brought him a woman caught committing adultery, they asked if she should be stoned according to the law of Moses. You probably remember what Jesus said to them.

> "If any one of you is without sin, let him be the first
> to throw a stone at her." John 8:7

Why does he do this? Because he knows we all have sinned. We all have broken the law, and we all deserve judgment and punishment. Yet his message was to show that even though we deserve death, God offers us life. We all have earned the death sentence from God because of our sin, and so Jesus points out to those who would condemn this woman that they too are like her. Jesus makes this point again in Matthew 7.

> Do not judge, or you too will be judged. For in the
> same way you judge others, you will be judged, and
> with the measure you use, it will be measured to
> you.

It would seem to be in our best interests, therefore, to not be judgmental of others. Sometimes we can be so distracted by other people's sins that we forget about our own. No matter how hard we try, no matter how good we act, no matter how much we pray and give to the poor, we still are in need of God's salvation and Jesus' gift to us. We still are sinners, and without God we would be completely lost and doomed.

Paul writes in I Corinthians:

"Do not go beyond what is written." Then you will not take pride in one man over against another. For who makes you different from anyone else? What do you have that you did not receive? And if you did receive it, why do you boast as though you did not? I Cor 4:7

And also in Ephesians:

For it is by grace you have been saved, through faith—and this not from yourselves, it is the gift of God— not by works, so that no one can boast. Ephesians 2:8-9

We received the gift of God that makes us saved, not through any work we have done to be good. So there is no reason to brag, and no reason to think that you are any better than any other person, even a *sinner*. A person who looks down on another because they think they are 'less sinful' is guilty of the sin of pride.

Jesus told a parable:

To some who were confident of their own righteousness and looked down on everybody else, Jesus told this parable: "Two men went up to the temple to pray, one a Pharisee and the other a tax collector. The Pharisee stood up and prayed about himself: 'God, I thank you that I am not like other men—robbers, evildoers, adulterers—or even like this tax collector. I fast twice a week and give a tenth of all I get.'
"But the tax collector stood at a distance. He would not even look up to heaven, but beat his breast and said, 'God, have mercy on me, **a sinner**.'
"I tell you that this man, rather than the other, went home justified before God. For everyone who exalts himself will be humbled, and he who humbles himself will be exalted." - Luke 18: 9-14

Again Jesus is speaking to those who think they are better than "sinners." If you do a search for the word "sinner" in the NIV version of the Bible, you will find that a lot of the New Testament uses of the word have to do with those who are looking down on sinners in their pride. This illustrates that it was an important message of the new Christian church that we should not look down on or judge others. It was important to Jesus, and the apostles.

Has the church lost this teaching? In many ways, I believe the answer is yes. However the problem goes even farther than that. Many people are categorized as 'sinners' just because they do not fit in with the American Church culture. For instance, if you don't wear nice button up shirts and dress cleanly all the time, you automatically must be a sinner. The hypocrisy extends from sin arrogance to an even further level of segregation. Now people who just look or act different must be sinners because they don't do things the "right way." This is the beginning of legalism. Legalism can be defined in many ways, but one of the simplest ways is to say that it is taking faith and making it about following rules and laws. It takes away the relationship with God, and instead puts in its place a heavy tome of regulations that one must obey to be a "good Christian." The sad part is, most of these rules have little or nothing to do with God.

We have learned what we should not do from Jesus. We should not judge, and should not think of ourselves better than others. So then, what should we do? We should repent from this way of looking at the world. Repent from this perspective of segregation of people into different levels of goodness. Once we turn away from this, and see all people the same, as God does, then we can truly love them. Without the judgment in our hearts in the way, we can then reach out to those around us. We are no better than anyone else, and we still sin. Once we realize this, we can do what Jesus said:

> How can you say to your brother, 'Let me take the speck out of your eye,' when all the time there is a plank in your own eye? You hypocrite, first take the plank out of your own eye, and then you will see

clearly to remove the speck from your brother's eye.
Matt 7:4-5

First, look at yourself and know who you are. A sinner, who has
done nothing to earn salvation from God. You have been given the
free gift of salvation. Then, once you see clearly, you can help
your brother. Notice Jesus mentions a plank (really big) in our own
eye versus a speck (pretty small) in our brother's eye. This should
keep us humble, and help us to realize that when we look at our
own sin we should see *more* of it in ourselves than we see in
others. When we start seeing people in love, and not looking for
their sin, we will truly be like the Christians that Jesus wanted us to
be; loving others, not judging them.

Who will listen to the message?

Jesus sought out those who would listen to his message.

> While Jesus was having dinner at Matthew's house,
> many tax collectors and "sinners" came and ate with
> him and his disciples. When the Pharisees saw this,
> they asked his disciples, "Why does your teacher eat
> with tax collectors and 'sinners'?"
> On hearing this, Jesus said, "It is not the healthy
> who need a doctor, but the sick." Matt 9:10-12

The people who need God the most are those who have been hurt
the most by the world, and sin. They have been hurt by their own
sin and the sin of others; they are sick. We all of course are sick to
a degree since we all have sin. Remember a time when you were
very sick or very injured. You felt terrible, and you didn't know
when it would stop. You would have welcomed any cure that
would help, even if it meant standing on your head ten minutes
every hour, you would do it just to get away from the pain. Now
think about when you had a minor cold or a small cut. You hardly
paid any attention to it at all. You could go about your life without
thinking much of this small problem.
      Earlier we talked about how many factors influence who a
person becomes in this life. Part of that was their life experience,

and that includes their suffering. If you have suffered much you are looking for a way to make it stop. People who are outcasts often become that way because they were rejected by others, and rejection hurts. They have felt alone for years in a society that will never accept them, perhaps for only *one thing* they may have done. These are the people Jesus went to. Jesus went to the outcasts, the freaks. Part of the reason is because these people were the ones more willing to hear the gospel. Think about America today. Most people in some way have heard something of the gospel message, some of it right and some wrong. Yet, what people does the church spend most of their time talking to? We have our little outreaches, maybe picnics or church events. But what kind of people will mostly come to those things? The *normal* people. If you think about it, the church mostly reaches out to the mainstream of society, and that mainstream has probably heard the gospel message over and over again.

What if churches began to target the freaks, the outcasts of society? Mostly these people's experience with the church and believers is one of rejection or condemnation. They don't feel welcome. In fact, it has been my experience in many subcultures that when someone in that culture finds out I am a Christian they immediately get defensive. They *expect* Christians to judge them. What if, for once, a Christian didn't pay attention to their weirdness, but just treated them like a person? Talked to them about what *they* like, about where they are at in life?

In the young adult service I visit at my church, pastor Jeff was talking about witnessing to others. He pointed out that we have done it the *same way* for decades. We submit the plan for salvation in simple terms, perhaps even mention the Four Spiritual Laws. People are so used to the same message that they immediately turn it off. People who are different, the outcasts and the freaks, think differently than the average person. Without knowing about them and their culture, how can we witness to them on a level they will understand? How can we meet them where we are unless we have some freaks ourselves that are *in* the culture? If we take anyone who becomes a Christian and make them into a cookie-cutter copy, how can they go back to their old culture and share their faith? It will be like they are speaking another language. When Paul preached the gospel, he spoke differently depending on

his audience. To the Jews he referred to the Old Testament
scriptures, because that is what they believed in. But when Paul
went to the Greeks, his message was completely different.

> While Paul was waiting for them in Athens, he was
> greatly distressed to see that the city was full of
> idols. So he **reasoned** in the synagogue with the
> Jews and the God-fearing Greeks, as well as in the
> marketplace day by day with those who happened to
> be there. -- Acts 17:16-17

The Greeks were strongly influenced by philosophy and debate in
their culture, so Paul goes to them and reasons with them. He even
visits the Areopagus, where people gathered to talk about and
listen to new ideas. He got up and spoke to them there:

> Men of Athens! I see that in every way you are very
> religious. For as I walked around and looked
> carefully at your objects of worship, I even found an
> altar with this inscription: TO AN UNKNOWN
> GOD. Now what you worship as something
> unknown I am going to proclaim to you.
>   The God who made the world and everything in it
> is the Lord of heaven and earth and does not live in
> temples built by hands. And he is not served by
> human hands, as if he needed anything, because he
> himself gives all men life and breath and everything
> else. -- Acts 17:22-25

Paul immediately appeals to *their* culture, *their* religion, *their*
temples. He references their belief in an unknown God. He
continues giving his message in terms the Greeks will understand:

> From one man he made every nation of men, that
> they should inhabit the whole earth; and he
> determined the times set for them and the exact
> places where they should live. God did this so that
> men would seek him and perhaps reach out for him
> and find him, though he is not far from each one of

us. 'For in him we live and move and have our
being.' As some of your own poets have said, 'We
are his offspring.'

"Therefore since we are God's offspring, we should
not think that the divine being is like gold or silver
or stone—an image made by man's design and skill.
In the past God overlooked such ignorance, but now
he commands all people everywhere to repent. For
he has set a day when he will judge the world with
justice by the man he has appointed. He has given
proof of this to all men by raising him from the
dead. (v26-31)

Paul refers to their own poetry! Can you imagine a Christian going
out from their church to witness to a group of hippies and asking to
read their poetry? Or taking a line from a depressing Goth poem
and finding a way that it points to God? Yet this is the equivalent
of what Paul does. He doesn't speak like he does to the Jews,
telling them about how Jesus was the Messiah of the Old
Testament; it would mean little or nothing to them. He instead
speaks to them from their own culture and gives them the message
in terms they can understand.

We have fields ripe for harvest in the outcasts of the world,
yet we don't reach out to them or just *don't know how to*. Imagine
if the church in America and all over the world started to learn
about these subcultures, how to speak to them, and went out and
told them about God. Imagine if once these freaks came to church
they weren't told that they couldn't have pink hair, or listen to rock
music, or play role playing games, and instead were encouraged to
have a real relationship with God. Then, those people that were
saved as freaks could go out and speak to others like them, sharing
the message of God in a language that would be understood. We
would see a church explosion like never seen before! That is, if the
church would open the doors and let it be known that the freaks are
welcome there.

Chapter 4

Legalism

Something that the church has always been vulnerable to is legalism. What is legalism? We see legalism show up in many places in the Bible, but in its most basic form, legalism is taking rules and regulations and making them the most important thing about one's faith. At its worst, it can reduce the Christian life to a list of things that one must do every day and make the Christian walk into slavery. It makes living "by the rules" the best and greatest part of faith, and forgets about the spirit and relationship with God.

I believe it is human nature for us to want to know "the right way" to do things. As Christians, we would love for there to be a list of things to do that will make us "good" or "acceptable" to God. It is also human nature for us to want to have the answers for everything. It is so hard for us to admit sometimes that we simply do not know something. How many men refuse to ask for directions because they simply do not want to admit, to a stranger, in front of someone else, that they don't know where they are? Scientists crave knowledge, and create theories to explain things we do not understand, because we so desperately want to know the answers.

Somehow, along the way, it has become the picture of the "perfect Christian" to have all the answers. We so badly want rules and black and white guidelines that we can forget that each person, each situation is unique. We take the words of the Bible and extend them, make them into little fences around every issue so we can compartmentalize life and organize it and say, "Ah yes, this fits here." It makes us feel better. The beginning of legalism is taking things from the Bible that were not meant to be rules and making them into rules.

What is a good example of this? Let's look at some things Paul said in his letter to the Thessalonians.

Be joyful always; pray continually – I Thess 5

Paul said to be joyful always. Therefore, we must be joyful. Always. If you are sad, you are breaking this rule, so you are sinning. Oh, and you have to pray all the time too. Did you pray all day today? If you didn't pray, continually, all day, you are sinning as well, according to this verse.

Of course, that is not what it really means. This would be not only legalistic but extremely literal in interpretation. We have to use some common sense and context when reading the Bible. Other verses and chapters should be examined on any subject you are studying to get a complete picture of what the Bible says. I could easily break off on a tangent here on how to study the Bible, but let us get back to the subject.

A second, even worse type of legalism is when it takes part of the Bible, assumes something about it and *adds to it*. This, I believe, comes from a desire to know the answers and be right, but also out of a desire to be righteous in other people's eyes. I have seen this type of legalism a lot. It has wounded me and Christians all over the world. The real problem with this type of legalism is that the rules are not only applied to the person who follows them, but they are applied to everyone else. And so the legalist must convert everyone to their way of doing things, because somehow it has become the *right* and *only* way to do things.

I have encountered many forms of legalism in my time, but the most pronounced was with a church I was a member of for many years. The legalism there was very subtle, yet, it was strong. This church, which I will call the Example Legalistic Church, or XLC, had two types of members. There were the members who had "seen the light" and were following all the "wise suggestions" that the church offered. Then there were the rest of the member who still hadn't had their "eyes opened" and were looked upon as literally, second class Christians. The "wise suggestions" were all the extra rules that they added to Christianity.

In fact, the XLC felt they were so correct in all their doctrines, they looked down and even felt pity for Christians they met that were in other denominations. The XLC was "charismatic" in their doctrine, and any other Christians who did not have the Baptism in the Holy Spirit were definitely second class, spiritually handicapped Christians. Not that anyone in XLC would ever say this outright; you would just see a sad shake of the head, or a sigh when the others were referred to. When you first went to XLC you would be greeted with many smiles. They had a newcomer class you could take, with refreshments and literature. You would feel very welcome for your first few visits.

Then, after a few weeks, people would start to ask you why you weren't more involved. Perhaps you should start attending homegroups, they might suggest. Homegroups are great for Christian growth, don't you know? Or you could join one of the ministry teams; the worship team, prayer team, missions team, or the new members team. They would tell you that *true* Christians are involved with their church. If you didn't join any ministries and kept attending week after week you would notice a change. People would ask you for a while if you were joining the groups, and which ones. If you still did not join one, after a while, someone would have a "talk" with you.

The talk would include the word "should" a lot. It probably would also include asking what your motivations in your heart were for not joining these ministries at church. Was this a sinful response perhaps? Probably the word "wise" would be used in the context of making wise decisions for your life. Was it wise to not grow as a Christian?

Either way, once you go to homegroup, which is a weekly evening meeting for prayer and study, you would start to learn other things. Now, homegroups by themselves I think are just fine, don't get me wrong. But in this case, if you weren't going to one you were not being a "good Christian." If you had children, and they were in public school, people would ask you, "Why don't you homeschool your children? Don't you really love them?" This is a real question that was asked of someone in a homegroup. They were basically accused of not loving their children because they sent them to public school, for whatever reason. This mother broke down to tears after being confronted about homeschooling this way.

In the homegroups you would learn that you needed to pray every day. If you didn't pray every day, what was wrong with you? Don't you have enough time for God? What sin is getting in the way of your prayer time? Is it really wise to not pray sometimes? Again, another rule is added. Dating was also frowned upon.

Classes and books on an alternative – courtship – were all through the church. Dating was "of the world" and therefore the sinful and wrong way to do things. Courtship was based on solid biblical principles, and it was the "wise" way to do things. If you were just dating, what was the motivation in your heart?

Once you made it to the first class of Christians at XLC, you then were subject to more scrutiny about all the unwritten rules. If you went to your homegroup and were part of a ministry at the church, then anyone there at anytime could come up to you and ask the motivation of your heart about, well, anything you said or did. If a male wore an earring, what was his motivation? Attracting attention to himself? Well, that is pride. If a male gave a female a – God forbid! – full frontal hug, well, that was completely "inappropriate", another favorite legalism word. No, you had to do the proper "Christian hug" for inter-sex hugging, from the side, or the girl had to make absolutely sure that her breasts did not so much as brush up against the male. Soon everything you did was weighed and measured, the motivations of your heart guessed at, even assumed.

One time I sang a "special music" as we Christians like to call it, during the service. I performed a song by a popular contemporary Christian artist, and I put a lot of my heart and soul into the performance; it was very lively and I moved around the stage a lot. Afterwards, I was told by the pastor that it was too showy and I was obviously drawing attention to myself because of pride. Of course, he didn't ask if I *felt* proud. He already "knew" somehow that my motivations were sinful. The XLC is the same church I mentioned earlier, where when I felt anxious I told my pastor about it who then replied that "anxiety is a sin." Black and white. No exceptions for individual situations. Everyone is nicely compartmentalized and ordered. We have all the answers. Yet, in the XLC, we have no freedom in Christ.

Can you see where the rules were added to the Bible? We are told to pray, yes, but nothing in the Bible says "have a quiet prayer time every day or you are sinning." And there certainly isn't anything that says, "Dating is a sin, you must court," yet this is how the XLC members acted. A problem we see here with legalism is it takes everyone and makes them the same, it makes all the extra rules the same for everyone, and individuality is lost.

I went to this XLC for over four years. At the end of my time there, I was exactly like them. You see, I wanted to be a pastor, so I had to be in the first category of Christians there, not the spiritually deprived second class. I wanted to go to their pastor's school. To do this, I had to be everything they wanted me to be. I lost almost all of who I was in that mold. I dressed plainly, modestly – now I would even say, boringly. I changed how I talked to match the way everyone else talked. I let anyone and everyone come up to me and question the motives for anything they wanted to ask me about. I believed the lie that the XLC was the most right, the best church and that all other Christians didn't quite measure up. Even though I am a disorganized person, I tried to pray every day. I tried to be "wise" and "appropriate" in all my dealings with others. I became almost no fun at all. I couldn't even say words like "wuss" because *you know* where *that* word comes from. I could no longer be creative and artistic because that was drawing attention to myself, and prideful. I love to make people smile and laugh, but instead I became much quieter because I was afraid that it was pride that motivated me, since they said so it must be true. I squashed the real me into this XLC mold until it strained at my very mind and spirit.

It was at this point I started to unravel. I started to feel like everyone was watching me, and waiting for my sin to show up. I felt like I would never, ever be good enough to go to the pastor's college. This was when I told my pastor about my anxiety problems and was told it was a sin. And so I became even more anxious; lying in bed with my heart pounding, thinking about how I was sinning by being anxious, then worrying even more. I had learned all the answers for everything. I knew theology back and forth, and had read numerous Christian books on many subjects. Yet my relationship with God and my Christian life were based on my performance, my ability to live up to a set of rules. Rules, I might add, that Jesus never meant us to live by.

Soon my anxiety became so bad I had to leave the church. I started visiting other churches, but I would have anxiety attacks during the service. I could imagine everyone around me seeing how sinful I was, watching me. For two years, I could not bear to go to church. Every time I tried to have a quiet prayer time, the anxiety would get so bad I could not even concentrate – because I associated praying with a rule I had to obey, not with my relationship with God. I had suppressed my real personality for so long my mind was worn down by the strain. I had started off with such faith and hope, yet legalism took all the life out of my walk with God and left me an empty, broken shell, unable to even turn to God for fear of all my failings.

My heart goes out to others that have gone through this experience. I can only hope that the grace of God kept you in the faith that you may be restored. I am still being restored from my experiences; God is faithful.

This type of teaching is not only damaging, it also turns people away from God and spirituality. That is why, I believe, Jesus spoke out against legalism so often and so strongly in the Bible.

> Then Jesus said to the crowds and to his disciples:
> "The teachers of the law and the Pharisees sit in
> Moses' seat. So you must obey them and do
> everything they tell you. But do not do what they
> do, for they do not practice what they preach. They
> tie up heavy loads and put them on men's shoulders,
> but they themselves are not willing to lift a finger to
> move them. -- Matt 23:1-4

The heavy loads were all the rules they gave to people. Matthew 23 is mostly a monologue where Jesus warns the Pharisees about their legalistic ways.

> Woe to you, teachers of the law and Pharisees, you
> hypocrites! You shut the kingdom of heaven in
> men's faces. You yourselves do not enter, nor will
> you let those enter who are trying to! -- v 13

Here we see Jesus showing that their legalism drives people away from the kingdom of heaven, or even worse – makes people feel like they could never get in!

> Woe to you, teachers of the law and Pharisees, you
> hypocrites! You give a tenth of your spices—mint,

dill and cummin. But **you have neglected the more
important matters of the law—justice, mercy
and faithfulness**. You should have practiced the
latter, without neglecting the former. You blind
guides! You strain out a gnat but swallow a camel.

The more important matters become neglected in legalism, and the
focus becomes on rules. Jesus shows them how nitpicky they are
by saying they are so concerned about these tiny issues they will
strain out something as small as a gnat, yet so ignorant of the larger
issue of what is important they end up swallowing a camel. An
analogy today would be like picking a piece of lint out of your
soup but leaving in a dead rat to eat!

> You are like whitewashed tombs, which look
> beautiful on the outside but on the inside are full of
> dead men's bones and everything unclean. In the
> same way, on the outside you appear to people as
> righteous but on the inside you are full of hypocrisy
> and wickedness. --v 27,28

When we become legalists, like the people from the XLC, we are
so concerned with appearance that we make it our God. We neglect
the important things, loving others, mercy and God's grace. We
become poisoned and corrupt in our legalism though we may look
wonderful on the outside. As I said, I believe it is human nature to
want to make laws to know exactly what is wrong and right.
However, when these rules become as important as God himself,
and more important than individual people, we destroy what the
rules were for and they cease to be good and become evil instead.
God commanded for us to keep the Sabbath holy in the Ten
Commandments. Yet the Pharisees added to this rule. They made
exact requirements; lists of what you could and could not do and if
you did one bit more – you were sinning. For instance the Bible
says not to do work on the Sabbath. The Pharisees decided they
had to define exactly what work was so you would have a clear
line to cross. This is part of what they came up with in their
Talmud, the laws followed in Jesus' time, as part of a definition of
"work":

"weaving two threads, separating two threads (in
the warp), tying a knot, untying a knot, sewing on
with two stitches, tearing in order to sew together
with two stitches..." (Tract Sabbath, Book I,
Chapter 7)

They even had restrictions on how far you could walk on the
Sabbath. Jesus went right after them for this kind of teaching. We
will look at two specific instances where Jesus dealt with the
Pharisees on this issue. First, in Matthew 12.

Going on from that place, he went into their
synagogue, and a man with a shriveled hand was
there. Looking for a reason to accuse Jesus, they
asked him, "Is it lawful to heal on the Sabbath?" He
said to them, "If any of you has a sheep and it falls
into a pit on the Sabbath, will you not take hold of it
and lift it out? How much more valuable is a man
than a sheep! Therefore it is lawful to do good on
the Sabbath." Then he said to the man, "Stretch out
your hand." So he stretched it out and it was
completely restored, just as sound as the other. But
the Pharisees went out and plotted how they might
kill Jesus. (v 11-14)

The laws for the Sabbath were so strict they even believed that
someone should not be healed on that day! Yet Jesus showed the
meaning, the spirit of the commandment: How much more
valuable is a man than a sheep? We are valuable to God. The rules
are not as valuable as we are. He makes this clear in Mark 12.

One Sabbath Jesus was going through the
grainfields, and as his disciples walked along, they
began to pick some heads of grain. The Pharisees
said to him, "Look, why are they doing what is
unlawful on the Sabbath?"
He answered, "Have you never read what David
did when he and his companions were hungry and

in need? In the days of Abiathar the high priest, he
entered the house of God and ate the consecrated
bread, which is lawful only for priests to eat. And
he also gave some to his companions." Then he said
to them, "The Sabbath was made for man, not man
for the Sabbath. So the Son of Man is Lord even of
the Sabbath." (v 24-28)

The rules were made for our good. As soon as they were taken and
made to do us harm, Jesus says we should not listen to them!
David ate the consecrated bread. He was hungry, he needed food
and so did his friends. The people's need became more important
than the law, because at that moment the law was not serving
David, it was hindering him. Now this does not mean to throw out
all the laws, but it shows they were meant for our good. It also
shows that each situation depends on the circumstances. We can't
just apply them all black and white, all the time. Jesus himself
shows this when he tells about David and his men. The laws are
made for *us,* we are not servants to the laws. As soon as we put the
laws before people we put the cart before the horse. The laws were
meant to be good for mankind.

I have seen another extreme example of legalism in terms
of marriage. This takes the verses on marriage and makes them
extreme and unwavering – even when a marriage becomes harmful
to a Christian. We just saw that Jesus showed that the laws are for
our good, and we can use our head and our hearts. Of course we
can save an animal from the ditch on the Sabbath, and of course we
can pray for someone's healing even though this might seem like
"work" in a strict sense. Jesus spoke about divorce and said,

"It has been said, 'Anyone who divorces his wife
must give her a certificate of divorce.' But I tell you
that anyone who divorces his wife, except for
marital unfaithfulness, causes her to become an
adulteress, and anyone who marries the divorced
woman commits adultery." – Matt 5:31-32

Let me ask you, if a woman is married to a man who beats her,
forces her to have sex with him whenever he wants, lies to her and

treats her horribly, is she forced to stay with him just because he calls himself a "Christian?" Is she doomed to be an "adulteress" just because she escaped a terribly abusive relationship? What do you think Jesus would say? We just saw him chastise the Pharisees for interpreting the Sabbath too strictly, would he not say that the laws were meant for our good, not for evil?

I hate to say this but I have found that there are churches that are so serious about this unbending "law" they have created, that an abused woman is forced to stay with her husband as long as he wants to keep her. If she left him and filed for divorce, get this, *she* would be kicked out of the church. Some churches call it excommunication. Can you see how ridiculous this is? However if a different woman in this same church committed adultery and her husband divorced her, she would be *forgiven* for the adultery and allowed to stay in the church. Plus her husband would be excused because his wife was an adulteress. In one instance we have an adulteress who can have a divorce and be forgiven and accepted in the church, and the other an abused, tortured woman who will be driven out if she takes action to protect herself. Something is seriously wrong in churches these days where this happens.

What we should get from what Jesus taught is that the meaning of the laws themselves must be understood in a way that keeps in mind the benefit to Christians. Jesus would not necessarily say to break the commandment, "Keep the Sabbath Holy", but he would have us see the law in the proper context. Even in the Old Testament God was displeased with Israel for strictly keeping the laws, yet not doing what is right. In fact, Jesus references the book of Hosea in the Matthew account of the Sabbath story above:

> If you had known what these words mean, 'I desire mercy, not sacrifice,' you would not have condemned the innocent. For the Son of Man is Lord of the Sabbath." Matt 12:7-8

The words quoted reference the Old Testament sacrifices required by law. What does God care about more? Having mercy on others, not the law itself. The law itself is a good thing, until it is used to hurt others. Then it becomes twisted against itself to condemn the innocent.

A sad truth is that many of our churches today there is legalism. We have rules about our rules. We do the same exact thing that the Pharisees did that Jesus chastised them for. When researching this chapter, I literally found two articles in my search results from Christians who are *advocating* the exact thing the Pharisees were in the above example. They list rules about how far you can travel on the Sabbath, about how you cannot cook and cannot work and they define exactly what work is, once again. Even in less strict churches, something has become sacred that is not from the Bible, and that is *tradition*.

Jesus also addresses this with the Pharisees, in Matthew 15. They asked him:

> Why do Your disciples break the tradition of the elders? For they do not wash their hands when they eat bread."
> And He answered and said to them, "Why do you yourselves transgress the commandment of God for the sake of your tradition?" (v 2-3)

Tradition. The idea that "this is the way we always have done things, and this is the way we always should do things." This is the kind of thing that can kill a church.

> These people honor me with their lips,
>   but their hearts are far away.
>   Their worship is a farce,
>   for they replace God's commands with their
> own man-made teachings (v 8-9)

Tradition can become so important to us that it can not only interfere with God's work but it can stifle it altogether. When I was in college I had the privilege of being an assistant to a pastor at a small country church. He had just recently joined this church and was trying to help the church grow. The deacons at that church, however, had been there a long, long time. They were well-respected and known in that little church, which had had the same thirty or forty members for the past decade, if not longer. The same lady played piano, they used the same worn out hymnals, and the same ushers took the collection every week. They had a picnic every summer, and business meetings every month. This new pastor, I will call him Dr. C, looked at what he saw and realized the church was stifling. People occasionally would visit but would not stay. So, Dr. C started changing things. He had me play guitar for a few of the songs, modern praise choruses mixed in with the old hymns on the piano. He started having meetings outside the church, at public places, talking with people. It was not long until we had a good crop of new folks coming to the church. I was happy to see the church growing and reaching new people. Yet the deacons were infuriated. Dr. C was changing their long held *traditions!* How dare he?

The status quo was so important to these deacons that they did not hesitate to go against him and tell lies about him. They began to call up members of the congregation and spread rumors. He was single and had a female friend he visited, so they began to plant seeds of sexual immorality about him. I don't even know what all they said but soon half of the congregation was ready to throw him out. Literally some members were ready to be violent.

Violence, for what? The sake of traditions? To keep their traditions, yes, and also their power. I am not going to say that Dr. C was sinless, but you can see how this situation is similar to what happened with Jesus and the Pharisees. Jesus was a threat to their power. He took away all the rules and laws they oppressed people with and made them free. In the same way, the deacons controlled the church by having only members that agreed with them in the congregation. Once Dr. C brought in new people who liked the changes, they would not side with the deacons.

Finally this conflict came to an ugly head. There was a church meeting called, and a vote taken. At that point, there were almost as many new members as there were old. One man actually was hoping to get a chance to beat up Dr. C in the parking lot afterwards. Both sides spoke, and the accusations flew. All the deacons were against Dr. C. They took a vote, not only to remove Dr. C but to basically get rid of all the new people, who would not want to stay without him. When the vote was taken, the majority decided he would be removed.

I remember afterwards in the parking lot, the two sides gathered on opposite ends, and I could hear the deacons' group all singing together, "Victory in Jesus." It left a bitter taste in my mouth, I can say. I went over to talk to them, because through all of this I had tried to be a mediator between both sides. As I walked up to them, one lady accused me of being there to "spy on them" for the "other side."

All of this happened, for what? A love of tradition. In the end, the church was back to its thirty members, with its same ushers and piano player, and nothing that was alive. The church had actually gone through a number of pastors in the past, continuing this cycle. They would not change, therefore they would not grow. Tradition was more important to them than love, than God's work, and to some of them, maybe more important than Christ himself, though I cannot see their hearts. I remember driving home that night, the moon was large and red in the sky, and I was thinking that whatever this was, it was not a victory for Jesus.

Chapter 5

Living by Grace

Most people know that the term gospel refers to the "good news" of salvation preached by Jesus Christ. That message was simple: repent and believe.

> After John was put in prison, Jesus went into Galilee, proclaiming the good news of God. "The time has come," he said. "The kingdom of God is near. Repent and believe the good news!" – Mark 1:14-15

What was the good news? Well, we often see the verse John 3:16 at sporting events, and many of us know that it says God gave us Jesus his only Son, and that whoever believes in him will have eternal life. That was and is the gospel message, the good news that God offers forgiveness and eternal life through his son.

This was what Jesus came and died for. This was his message. And it was given to us, as the church, to tell others this good news. Somewhere along the way it seems that many individuals and churches have lost sight of the centrality, the overarching importance of the gospel message. Other issues have become so important that they are either equal to or overshadow the gospel message completely.

Paul was concerned when he spoke to the Galatians about their losing sight of the original gospel message. In Galatians chapter 1, we can see he is very serious about what he sees happening there.

> I am astonished that you are so quickly deserting the one who called you by the grace of Christ and are turning to a different gospel— which is really no gospel at all. Evidently some people are throwing you into confusion and are trying to pervert the gospel of Christ. But even if we or an angel from heaven should preach a gospel other

> than the one we preached to you, let him be
> eternally condemned! As we have already said, so
> now I say again: If anybody is preaching to you a
> gospel other than what you accepted, let him be
> eternally condemned! – v. 6-9

There are so many "different gospels" out there that people end up following. The gospel of "baptism by immersion", or the gospel of "courtship", the gospel of "pro-life", or maybe the gospel of "you should dress like we do or else." Not all of these things are bad things, but none of them are the gospel. When telling everyone about your pro-life rally becomes more important then telling them about Christ, what happened to the gospel? When you are trying to "save" someone from the horrible, evil practice of "dating", isn't there something you should be more concerned about? Perhaps their immortal soul?

In the case of the Galatians, above, the Jewish believers were trying to enforce all the Jewish laws and customs on the non-Jewish (Gentile) believers. They made being a Christian all about following laws, and not about following Jesus (see Galatians Chapter 2.) The gospel Paul talks about in this letter is from the calling of God by grace. This is not the only time the gospel is associated directly with grace in the Bible.

> However, I consider my life worth nothing to me, if
> only I may finish the race and complete the task the
> Lord Jesus has given me—the task of testifying to
> the gospel of God's grace. -- Acts 20:24

Paul, in his farewell here in Acts, says the gospel is "of God's grace." What is this grace that is associated with the gospel? Well, the gospel is the message that if we believe in Jesus, we will be given eternal life. The grace in the message is that though we were sinners, Christ died for us and paid for our sins. Grace is best described as "unmerited favor." A gift we did not earn. We certainly did not earn Christ dying for us. Yet he died, and not only that, because he died we are now able to spend eternity with God, living forever in peace and joy. Talk about unmerited favor! That is the grace that is in the gospel, extended to us from the true, living God.

The gospel is simple in its message. Believe in Jesus. Believe what? That he is God's son and that his death paid for our sins. If we believe he is God's son, and one with God then he also deserves our worship as God. We believe that he rose from the dead, and his resurrection is the promise and proof that we will rise also.

Twice in Galatians, Paul counters those who are adding rules to the gospel with the freedom we have in Christ.

> Galatians 2:4
> This matter arose because some false brothers had infiltrated our ranks to spy on the freedom we have in Christ Jesus and to make us slaves.

> Galatians 5:1
> It is for freedom that Christ has set us free. Stand firm, then, and do not let yourselves be burdened again by a yoke of slavery.

What is this freedom he speaks of? In the New Testament, Jesus clearly went against the teachings of the Pharisees and the teachers of the law at that time. Men were slaves, piled with burdens they could not carry. He preached that what was on the *inside* was more important than the *outside*. He said God cared what your heart was like, as opposed to what clothes you wore, or whether you washed your hands, or what you ate. So, what does this freedom look like? What does it mean to live by grace?

The Church of Grace

Whenever I mention living by grace, I am almost always met by the same reaction. "Why, you can't just let Christians go around without any rules! They will start sinning like mad! It will be an orgy of sin! We need to control people, help them fight their sin with the rules about what they shouldn't do! Without rules, they will turn away from God!"

Paul must have had a similar reaction also when he spoke about grace, given what he says in Romans 6:

> What then? Shall we sin because we are not under
> law but under grace? By no means! v.15

Neither Paul nor I would encourage you to sin because we have this freedom. The vision of the church of grace, as I see it, is one that grows closer to God in relationship.

I believe in many churches the cart is put before the horse in terms of trying to live holy lives. Rules will not bring us closer to God. Living a sinless life (if it were possible) will not bring us closer to God. Getting *closer to God* brings us closer to God. It is about a relationship. If someone wanted to be close to anything, they would spend time with whatever it was. To get close to God, you spend time with him. You talk to him. You listen. You think about the beauty, majesty, and power of God. You pray and worship, in whatever way God has given you to do so. And when you draw close to God, you will not want to sin, because you will respond out of love and out of the closeness of his Spirit. So, when we have relationship with God *first,* then a godly life proceeds out of that. That puts the horse and the cart where they belong.

A church full of grace would not be bound by our modern ideas of "how church is done." The church, first and foremost, is *the people of God.* As many in our modern church movements have said, "The church is NOT the building we meet in." We are the church. Everywhere we go, we are bringing God with us. We are part of a community of believers from all walks of life.

One of the aspects of a church of grace would be one that does not judge others. A person should feel welcome to come join the family of God and still be the unique, beautiful creation they were made to be. There wouldn't be a dress code, or a different Christian language. You wouldn't be told you had to pray exactly a certain way, or when to stand up and sit down. Your life's history would not be analyzed. Your CD collection wouldn't be inspected for what someone considers objectionable. It wouldn't just be friendly to freaks and outcasts; it would be friendly to everyone.

It is so hard to describe this church, because I know some may imagine complete chaos, and people running around doing whatever they wanted. That is not what I mean. What I mean is a church where they know what the most important two things are in life: God, and his children.

The church of grace would follow these words of Jesus:

> "Teacher, which is the greatest commandment in the Law?" Jesus replied: " 'Love the Lord your God with all your heart and with all your soul and with all your mind.' This is the first and greatest commandment. And the second is like it: 'Love your neighbor as yourself.' All the Law and the Prophets hang on these two commandments." Matt 22:36-40

If we do these two things, love God, and love each other, Jesus says that we will be fulfilling the laws. That's what God meant for us all along: for us to love God, and each other. We will love each other and rejoice in our salvation together. We will be *God* focused and *people* focused, not *sin* focused. We will know in our hearts how sinful we are, and be much less inclined to judge others, knowing the greatness of the sin in our own heart.

People will be free of the confinements of rules; they will realize that their personal revelations from God may not apply to everyone else. What do I mean by this? Let's look at an example. We are told in the Bible for instance, that women should dress modestly (I Tim 2:9.) We know modesty is different depending on your culture, but we could probably at least establish some boundaries, such as: going around naked would be too revealing, and wearing a floor length skirt is definitely modest since it shows nothing. So, somewhere in between there is where it changes. The question is where? The Bible certainly doesn't say "two inches above the knee, any more than that is sin." Now a person may have an idea of what is modest for herself, and that is fine. Yet, when that idea is made into a law that everyone else has to follow, that becomes legalism. In the church of grace, it would be okay if people had different ideas of where the line was, and they wouldn't try to push their idea of it onto everyone else. We would not worry about such things. Think about it, the beauty is that the other believers with you at the church are *already saved.* There is no urgent calling from Jesus to save them from their skirts being too short! Instead we can focus on the bigger issues of life; again, God and other people. Loving them.

When we start measuring everyone by the same rules, making everyone live by our opinions of what is right, we no longer are treating them as individuals. In the church of grace, we would see each situation and person looked at separately. People would not all be lumped into the same mold; they would be seen as individuals. Life is often too complex to make hard and fast rules about things. Some situations require consideration and thought, not being mashed into a mold. Think back to my old church where I had anxiety problems. I reached out for help about my anxiety, and was told "anxiety is a sin." Surely, it may be in certain situations. But is it in all situations? Should we simply turn our minds and hearts off, and not consider the person involved? Boxing everyone with a similar problem into the same category takes away individuality, respect, and love. Each person has reasons for what they do, and unless we care enough to find out those reasons, we really have no idea about who they really are.

The church of grace would have community; closeness to each other and closeness to God. We would think of others before ourselves, and get to know each other. We would focus on the good qualities of God, and how much we have been forgiven. Each person would be a unique gem, a different thread in the beautiful tapestry of God's family. Instead of wanting to change each other, we would want to get to know all the wondrous and unique gifts each one had been given by God. We would encourage each other to be who we really are in God, not to sin, but to grow in love and not be confined.

People are Individuals

Recently I heard a song by Third Day that typifies what happens often in the church today. People seem to be so eager to offer correction, advice, and admonishment. When you have an entire congregation always correcting each other, what type of response do you think it will generate? Have you ever seen the movie *Office Space*? Peter Gibbons, an office worker, forgets to fill out a new report that was mentioned in a recent memo. His boss meets him at the beginning of the day and asks him if he got

the memo about the TPS reports. He answers yes. Then his boss
tells him about the memo and how the TPS reports are important.
He says he knows, but he just forgot. Then the boss promises to get
him another copy of the memo, and he says he has one. He sits
down in his cubicle, and another boss calls him about the TPS
reports, and he has to go through the same conversation again. Yes,
he got the memo. Yes, he knows about the TPS reports. No, he
doesn't need another copy of the memo. Later in the film he runs
into another supervisor. Guess what he says? Yes, that's right: TPS
reports.

Imagine going to church where everyone feels it is their
duty to remind you of your shortcomings, your mistakes. After a
while you wouldn't even feel like going. You might respond with
some feelings that mirror what Third Day sings about in their song
How Do You Know.

You're thinking that you've got all the answers
You've got my situation figured out
But you're only seeing part of the picture
There's so much more that you don't know about

And here you come to speak your mind
But I'll say one more time

How do you know, how do you know
What I'm supposed to be doing
Why do you go, why do you go on
Thinking you know my fate
So many times I've lost my step
But never lost my way
How do you know, how do you know
When I don't know myself

When we fail to look at people as individuals, we can be tempted
to simplify their lives into clichés, or offer simple spiritual
platitudes as solutions. But each person is complex, with a history
and a different experience of life, and even God.

The church of grace would first be concerned with reaching
out in love for people struggling, not offering correction. We are

encouraged to give correction, but out of love. Loving someone enough to know their situation means we will not paint them into a box. Also we should know when to give correction. Above we saw an example of over-correction with the TPS reports. Just because you see a brother or sister stumbling does not mean God has appointed *you* to speak to them about it. If everyone thinks they should correct everyone else about everything, no one would have time to talk about anything else!

Personally, I invite people to speak to me about things in my life that I know and trust. These people also know me, my situation, and my life. If you are not one of the people I have invited to speak to me, I may just respond like the song, "How do you know what I'm supposed to be doing?"

Jesus many times in the Bible treated people in unique and different ways. Each situation was different, and we can see from his words he knew the other person. Remember the example of the woman at the well? The *Samaritan* woman at the well; he wasn't even supposed to talk to her, according to the "rules." He knew she had had five husbands. He told her that he was the Messiah and that he had living water for her to drink. (John 4) When he spoke to the young rich man, he told him to give up his riches to the poor. (Matthew 19) Soldiers asked him what to do and he said not to extort money, and not to accuse people falsely. Tax collectors asked and he said to only collect what they were required to. (Luke 4) To the woman in adultery he said she was not condemned and not to sin any more. (John 8) He also said that God knows us so well that he knows how many hairs are on our heads (Matthew 10.) God cares enough to know us each individually. Jesus had different things to say to different people, depending on what it was they needed to hear. Yes, he preached the gospel to everyone, but he did more – he got personal. He didn't walk around saying "Hey you," to everyone, he called them by name. "Zacchaeus," he said, "come down from that tree!" Each person was special to him. When the woman came and poured the expensive perfume on his head, the disciples condemned the waste, saying it could have been sold for money for the poor. Though this would make sense in most situations, this one was different.

> Jesus said to them, "Why are you bothering this
> woman? She has done a beautiful thing to me. The
> poor you will always have with you, but you will
> not always have me. – Matt 26: 10-11

Yes, in general it is good to help the poor. Yet this was a unique
situation. Jesus made an exception. How many times have we been
too stiff-necked to make an *exception* for someone who meant
good by something they have done? Each situation is unique, and
Jesus recognized that with this woman. So let us do the same!
Before we are ready to correct someone, let us first invest the time
to really know this person and their situation. Let us allow for a
different childhood, a different culture, a different experience with
God. Let's love them as a unique person, and not put them into a
cookie-cutter mold.

Not Happy Little Robots

The church I envision would be made up of a diverse group
of people. If you went to a gathering of these believers you would
see all kinds of people. I don't just mean different races of people,
but different types of people. You would look at this group and
think that it is the craziest gathering you have seen because none of
these people seem to have anything in common. Yet it would be
beautiful. There would be no 'dress code' for church. People there
would be dressed in clothes from their different countries and
cultures, you'd see some teens in ripped up jeans next to a Mom in
a pretty dress. Or heck, how about the Mom in ripped up jeans and
the teens in pretty dresses! People with tattoos and piercings would
walk among the crowd and be right at home alongside everyone
else. You'd see some folks with tie-dye shirts and flip flops and
people with hair every color of the rainbow. Yet they would all
have this in common: Christ. The church would be founded on the
two greatest commandments: loving God, and loving each other.
I spoke to a young man recently, Steve, who had visited a
church with his girlfriend. He said a couple took them in and

talked to them. The husband spoke to Steve about how their church was "diversified." I asked him what he thought that meant. Steve said, "Well, I saw that there were white people and black people there. So maybe that is what they meant." So then I asked, well, how did they all dress? "The same," he answered. So this church was proud of itself because it had two different races of people that all dressed the same. This was "diversified" to them.

People see Christians at church, and out in life. Now I know not all churches are like this, but many are. People see everyone dressing the same, talking the same, doing the same things. They see a bunch of happy little robots. Yes! We are Christians and we are all so happy in our little button down shirts and pretty dresses and could we pray for God to bless you? The impression that the non-believers will get from this is that we are *all the same.* And to become a Christian, they must turn into another Happy Little Robot. Let me ask you, do you think that is really appealing to a regular person off the street? Yes, please, I'd like to give up my uniqueness and differences and become a Happy Little Robot, thank you.

How do you think a freak would feel about coming to church? They don't see any other unusual people there, just the robots. So someone who is different would think, "They will never accept me this way. I don't want that." Imagine if instead they saw a church of lots of different people. One time I visited a church in Durham, NC and the pastor's son who was probably only about ten years old had a *blue mohawk.* That made me feel pretty good about being a goth visiting their church.

If we don't try to change these freaks when they come to church, then we will have diversity. If we don't put forth the mold of the Happy Little Robot, then the church will represent people from all cultures, and that makes it beautiful to God, but also appealing to those who are different. If a freak sees other freaks in a church, he can think, "Yes! I can be accepted there." In a recent email with Neil Cole, he quoted me a verse of Scripture, with a slight change:

> "Was a man a freak when he was called? Let him
> stay in that condition from which he was called." --
> 1 Corinthians 7:17-24

When someone comes to Christ, our concern should not be to make them like the rest of us Christians, as if God only wanted there to be one mold for every Christian. He made us all different and accepting that and accepting differences in people is what God meant for us all along. God's vision of the church is unity, it is all over the new testament. Here is one example:

> Therefore, as God's chosen people, holy and dearly loved, clothe yourselves with compassion, kindness, humility, gentleness and patience. Bear with each other and forgive whatever grievances you may have against one another. Forgive as the Lord forgave you. And over all these virtues put on love, which binds them all together in perfect unity. Col 3:11-14

We are encouraged here to forgive each other, which would be when we sin against each other. How much more should we accept differences, which are not of sin? Love is the key to unity. If we can love those that are different from ourselves, then we can live with them as a church.

Life in the Spirit

We have the Spirit of God within us, as Christians. How often do we realize that? Do we even sense that his Spirit is in us? However much we do sense it; He is there. Think about this for a second: God's Spirit lives inside you. Yes, even after what you have done today, or yesterday, or last week. We are made alive by God's spirit in us.

How often do we listen for the Spirit of God? Romans 8:14 says that those who are led by the spirit are the children of God. If we are God's children, then we will follow the leading of the Spirit. Yet, how many times do we try to work in our own wisdom without listening for the Spirit?

The new way of living in Christ is by the spirit, not by the law.

> You foolish Galatians! Who has bewitched you?
> Before your very eyes Jesus Christ was clearly
> portrayed as crucified. I would like to learn just one
> thing from you: Did you receive the Spirit by
> observing the law, or by believing what you heard?
> Are you so foolish? **After beginning with the
> Spirit, are you now trying to attain your goal by
> human effort?** Have you suffered so much for
> nothing—if it really was for nothing? Does God
> give you his Spirit and work miracles among you
> because you observe the law, or because you
> believe what you heard? -- Galatians 3:1-5

Once we become a Christian by God's grace and spirit, do we then tip our hats to God and say, "Thank you, I'll take it from here"? Life in the spirit requires change, it requires being challenged. If we order everything into neat little laws and boxes, making everything in black and white, decisions become easy. That doesn't mean those decisions are right. The walk with God is alive, it is one of the Spirit, and every day it is changing, every situation is one you face with God, relationally, with his Spirit. If we categorize everything into compartments, then why do we need the Spirit any more? We have already figured it all out, again, on our own, using our own minds. Some may say they are using logic, and God gave us logic and reason. This is true, but what good is logic and reason without love? And is our logic and reason as good as God's? God can see the whole picture in every situation, and I guarantee that will always include things we cannot see. So a life in the Spirit would involve a relational walk with God, praying and *listening* for his leading.

Relationship not Rules

The young man I mentioned earlier, Steve, told me more of his conversation with the man at the church he visited. He was invited over for dinner, and he said that not ten minutes after he arrived, the man pulled out his bible, set it on the table and asked, "What rules do you live by Steve? I bet they are a lot different than the ones in here." This is one of the very first things this man talked to Steve about. The Bible was demonstrated and used as a book of rules.

This is one of the worst things we can do as Christians. The Bible is a living, breathing story of God and his love and salvation for us, yet it is being turned into a "book of rules." This is perverse. It flies in the face of the message of Jesus, of his forgiveness and love. Let me ask you, do you think this made Steve want to come back to this church?

Steve also told me that as soon as the church members found out he and his girlfriend were living together, a lady took his girlfriend aside and spent a long time questioning her about this situation and telling her it was wrong. What is missing here? The *gospel* is missing. Steve and his girlfriend went to this church, and the church didn't even try to see if they were saved! They didn't present the gospel at first, the first thing they did was try to change them!

What does it mean to be a Christian? Jesus said in John 15:15, "I no longer call you servants, because a servant does not know his master's business. Instead, I have called you friends, for everything that I learned from my Father I have made known to you." We are friends of God. God gives us his spirit, more than that, he lives within us! How can he live within us yet we have no relationship with him? We are meant to walk with God, talk with God, and live by his Spirit. Jesus was an example of that. He knew his Father, he talked with him as one who is close, and he prayed for all believers to be one in him.

> I pray also for those who will believe in me through
> their message, that all of them may be one, Father,
> just as you are in me and I am in you. May they also
> be in us so that the world may believe that you have
> sent me. -- John 17:20-21

He prayed for us to be one, just as he was with God. He was specific as to how this would happen. That we would all be one just as CHRIST was in GOD. How close were they? So close, they could be called **one.** This relationship with God is intimate, it is close. We are to be one with God, as Jesus prayed.

Being a Christian, therefore, is not about rules, it is about a relationship. We don't need to puzzle out all the scriptures in our own strength and create a list of rules about being a Christian. How dead is that? There is no relationship, no life there. The scriptures come *alive* with the Spirit of God. "But the Counselor, the Holy Spirit, whom the Father will send in my name, will teach you all things and will remind you of everything I have said to you." (John 14:26) Every day we have the privilege of the presence of God with us. Yet I know myself I take it for granted. If only I could be more aware of God's Spirit in me! I pray that for myself and for you also, that we come closer to being truly one with our Lord.

In this relationship, we have the ability to see people through God's eyes, in the Spirit, and not by the law. We will have eyes of love, not of judgment. We will see others as God's unique creations. When we make decisions we will know that the Spirit of God is there to guide us. You may notice from time to time that a situation you are in is not clearly described in the Bible. How will you handle it? Perhaps you will want to reason it out, or take a Scripture that is vaguely related and use it as a rule. But you have the Spirit to guide you and open your eyes. You can pray, and seek guidance through others and the Bible, always holding on to the Spirit of God. One of the reasons God did not spell out every rule in the Bible is because he knows we would then use the Bible as a rulebook, and it would become our master. Instead, as Jesus said, the Sabbath and the laws are for our good. They serve *us*, we do not serve them. If we live by the Spirit in a relationship with God, a wonderful thing will happen: we will see everyone else as a unique individual and love them. No longer will we judge by appearance or small superficial things, instead we will live by love. Love will be first in our minds, truly, as Jesus continued in his prayer for us in John 17: "I have made you known to them, and will continue to make you known in order that the *love you have for me may be in them* and that I myself may be in them." The love of God can be in us. The perfect, accepting, love of God. The love of the gospel message that says even though we were sinners, God loved the world so much he died for us. He didn't ask us to change before he died – he did it first out of love. This church of grace that I envision is a community of believers diverse yet united together in Christ's love. This is the beautiful bride of Christ that the scriptures speak of.

Chapter 6

Giving up Arguments to Achieve Harmony

Sometimes I ask myself, "Why do we have so many denominations?" I'm sure most of us have given some thought to the question. I believe that, in general, having different types of churches is good and that denominations in and of themselves are not a bad thing. However, many denominations started because of a dispute, an argument even, about a particular point in scripture. For instance in the 1800's the Disciples of Christ church split over whether to allow piano and organ music in worship services. This led to the creation of the Churches of Christ. Not all splits were over such trivial issues – many of the splits in the 1800's were over the issue of slavery.

Still, many Christians identify themselves with their denomination. "I am a Baptist," or "I am a Presbyterian." This is actually similar to something that Paul talks about in first Corinthians.

> You are still worldly. For since there is jealousy and quarreling among you, are you not worldly? Are you not acting like mere men? For when one says, "I follow Paul," and another, "I follow Apollos," are you not mere men? What, after all, is Apollos? And what is Paul? Only servants, through whom you came to believe—as the Lord has assigned to each his task. I planted the seed, Apollos watered it, but God made it grow.   – I Cor 3:3-6

In the same way, I believe denominations are servants working for God. We can find God and do his work through the church we are part of. Yet, we should not see ourselves as anything but *Christians.* Paul continues on with his letter, "For we are God's fellow workers; you are God's field, God's building." (verse 9.) We are all *fellow* workers, together. We should be working together, not separating ourselves. We collectively are as Christians God's church, God's "building."

John Wesley, considered the founder of the Methodist church, made an appeal to Christians. He used an often quoted phrase by the early protestant church founders, "In essentials, unity; in non-essentials, liberty; in all things, charity." If only we kept these words in front of us today to guide us. Yet instead of liberty in Christ, we find division. Yes, there are some open-minded Christians, and yes, there are some whose minds are so open their brains fall out, as the saying goes. But because of our yearning desire to be "right" on every issue, we end up dividing ourselves over things that are not very important. This is a sad reality, since one of the strongest teachings of the New Testament is unity among all believers. As we saw in the last chapter, Jesus prayed for us all to be *one*. The "charity" spoken of by John Wesley is the love of the Father that Jesus prayed for. (In the King James Version of the Bible, love was often translated as "charity.") It has always been God's vision for us to be one together in love.

How do we do this? I believe one of the ways is to understand what Wesley and others were speaking of when they say "essentials" and "non-essentials." When I was facing my anxiety problems about church, I went to a Christian counselor. After discussing with me my problem, he drew a diagram similar to this on his whiteboard.

(see next page)

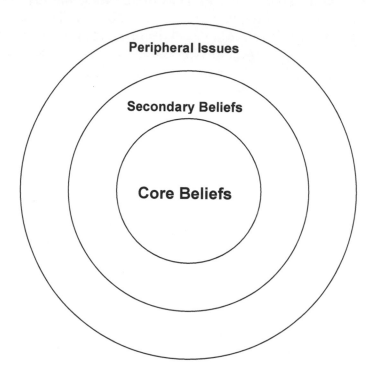

He said that as Christians, we all have certain beliefs that fall into different categories. What makes us all Christians is that we share our core beliefs. When we get outside the core beliefs, though we may have strong feelings or convictions about these other beliefs, we should not consider them "essentials." So yes, we can have these secondary beliefs, but to have unity in non-essentials, we must not let differences in these beliefs separate us from other Christians. The question then remains: what are the essentials?

I am not a great theologian like John Calvin, Augustine, or Wesley, but I believe the message of Christianity is meant for everyone. That means that God presented it in such a way that you don't have to be a great theologian or a literary genius to puzzle out the gospel message. In fact, the Bible says:

The foolishness of God is wiser than man's wisdom,
and the weakness of God is stronger than man's
strength. Brothers, think of what you were when

you were called. Not many of you were wise by
human standards; not many were influential; not
many were of noble birth. But God chose the
foolish things of the world to shame the wise; God
chose the weak things of the world to shame the
strong. - I Cor 1:25-27

So permit me to be foolish for a moment and try to enumerate what
I believe to be the essentials of Christianity.

God's plan for salvation

Jesus was the son of God, sent to die and pay the price for our sins.
Only through acceptance of his sacrifice and faith in him can we be
saved from eternal death. Jesus rose from the dead and lives
forever, and all people will rise from the dead to face judgment.
(John 3:16, John 14:6, Rev 20:12)

The Trinity

Jesus as the son of God is also God. God the Father, the Son and
the Holy Spirit have existed since the beginning as one. (2 Cor
13:14, Eph 2:18, John 1:1-4)

Heaven and Hell

There is a place of eternal life where believers will live with God
in peace, and there is also a place where those who do not choose
Christ will live forever without God in misery. (Luke 16:23, Mark
9:43, Rev 20:15, Rev 21:1-4)

The Bible contains the inspired words of God

The scriptures were written by people under the inspiration of the
Holy Spirit, and are God's words to us. (2 Tim 3:16, 2 Peter 1:20-
21)

Surely, there may be a few others that some might consider the
core beliefs, but I have tried to make them as simple as possible.

Why? Because I believe these are the things that *unite* us together as Christians. The key is not to let the *other* things outside of the core *divide* us. We can say as Christians that we believe in Jesus as our savior and our God. We believe he is the only way to salvation and that the words written in the Bible giving us this message are from God himself. The beauty and simplicity of the gospel message is apparent in the words from John 3:16, so often quoted… "For God so loved the world that he gave his only son, that whoever should believe in him will have eternal life." That is what brings us together and binds us. Why should we let quarrels about which version of the Bible, what music is played, what clothes we wear, or any other peripheral issue divide us?

For a moment let us talk about the second circle, the "secondary beliefs" as I have labeled them. They may be important doctrinal beliefs to you. How you feel about baptism, or the end times, or the role of a pastor in a church may seem important. You may know the Bible verses about these things, or at least, most of them. You may think you have your doctrine pretty solid. So, why do other people disagree with you? Most people don't consider the fact that they themselves might be wrong. Instead they think, "Well that person who disagrees with me just doesn't know scripture as well, or hasn't really heard from the Holy Spirit in that area." Why not think that maybe, just *maybe*, you don't have it all right. That you could possibly, dare I say it, be *wrong* about some of these things. I think part of learning how to be in unity with other believers is leaving the possibility open that you are indeed wrong about some of these beliefs that you may hold precious and dear to your heart.

Great Men Disagree

Sometimes when I feel that my stand on a certain issue might be right and obvious to everyone else I think: why do these other people disagree with me?! I remind myself that many great Christian theologians, writers, and saints had different ideas on these issues. People like John Calvin, who taught himself Hebrew and Greek and suffered physical ailments so bad that sometimes he had to be carried to the pulpit to preach. He wrote his own commentaries on the books of the Bible and many other works. His teachings were so prominent they were titled "Calvinism." Yet I can blithely disagree with Calvin, who taught infant baptism for the children of believers. Do I know as much as Calvin? He could read the scriptures in the original languages. No, obviously I don't. C.S. Lewis, who knew Latin and Greek by age six, wrote one of the most profound theological books of our time, *Mere Christianity*. Yet he believed in the evolution that Darwin taught, except that it was evolution by the hand of God, and that the creation story in the Bible therefore was not to be taken literally. John Wesley, founder of the Methodist church whom I mentioned before, disagreed with John Calvin on the issue of predestination. Calvin taught that only certain people were meant to be saved from the beginning of the world by God and nothing can change that, whereas Wesley taught that it was up to each person to choose or not to choose God. Both of these men knew much more about the scriptures than I do now, and probably more than I ever will know. Yet they disagree on this point. How can I, less educated than these men, choose between the two? In some ways, I do not have to. I can, in the grace of God admit that, "I don't know for sure." I can favor one or the other, and know my reasons why, but in the end can I really say definitively that I have it right? While I was researching this subject I came across a sermon by John Wesley. It is listed as his *Sermon 58, On Predestination*. This is, startlingly, just what I am talking about when he addresses this subject:

"Hard to be understood" we may well allow them to be, when we consider how men of the strongest understanding, improved by all the advantages of education, have continually differed in judgment concerning them. And this very consideration, that there is so wide a difference upon the head between men of the greatest learning, sense, and piety, **one might imagine would make all who now speak upon the subject exceedingly wary and self-diffident. But I know not how it is, that just the reverse is observed in every part of the Christian world. No writers upon earth appear more positive than those who write on this difficult subject.** *Nay, the same men, who, writing upon any other subject, are remarkably modest and humble, on this alone lay aside all self-distrust,*

And speak ex cathedrÿaa infallible.

This is peculiarly observable of almost all those who assert the absolute decrees. But surely it is possible to avoid this: **Whatever we propose, may be proposed with modesty, and with deference to those wise and good men who are of a contrary opinion;** *and the rather, because so much has been said already, on every part of the question, so many volumes have been written, that it is scarcely possible to say anything which has not been said before. All I would offer at present, not to the lovers of contention, but to men of piety and candour, are a few short hints, which perhaps may cast some light on the text above recited.*

Wesley basically says it baffles him that those who speak on this subject would be so absolute in their opinion one way or another, since many great and learned men have disagreed on the subject. Instead he finds contention, so he speaks not to those who love contention, but to men of piety. Let us be those who love unity more than contention. These secondary beliefs we have, I hope I can convince you, are non-essential. We should allow freedom and respect of those who disagree. What brings us together is so much more wonderful and glorious than the things that set us apart. Let us instead be like Paul when he came to the Corinthians and said, "When I came to you, brothers, I did not come with eloquence or superior wisdom as I proclaimed to you the testimony about God. For *I resolved to know nothing while I was with you except Jesus Christ and him crucified.*" (I Cor 2:1-2, emphasis mine.)

Personal Revelation

Have you ever had someone come to you and tell you about something they heard from God? It is not an unusual thing, as the Bible says the Holy Spirit is our teacher (John 14:26.) Sometimes this person starts telling everyone this revelation they had from God. However, this revelation may have been personal and only for them. God does deal with us as individuals in relationship with him, as we have seen. He may have a message just for us. For instance, the rich young man that talked with Jesus was told to give his riches to the poor. But Jesus didn't tell every rich man that! Sometimes God will reveal to us something in the Bible that clarifies a situation for us. However, that does not always mean that the revelation we received is for everyone else on the planet. Yes, it is exciting when we receive leading from the Spirit, and it is good to speak of it. Just remember that we have not suddenly become everyone's personal prophet on how to live or what to do if we receive a revelation.

Let's say that someone reads "pray without ceasing" as we mentioned before and feels inspired to have a personal prayer time every day. He starts doing it and is blessed by God. It is so great he goes out and tells everyone he knows that God says you should have a personal prayer time every day. Of course, there is nothing wrong with having a personal prayer time every day. Yet, not everyone has the same structure in their life. Someone in the military who is in a war may be too busy staying alive each day to sit down with the Bible and pray. Yet, this person can pray (and probably docs!) in brief moments he has between fighting for survival. A mother with four children whose husband just died may not have time to eat or sleep enough, let alone pray every day! We all are in different places in life, with different schedules and different responsibilities. Let us take each one as it comes and more importantly, let God deal with each of us individually. If I am in a relationship with God, I trust him to speak to me about things in my life. Perhaps I trust a select few others to speak for him as well. But a personal revelation for one person may not be one that applies to someone else. So I will listen, and be respectful, but if I don't do what you say, love me regardless. Or at least, respect my freedom as a Christian.

I want to say that there is nothing wrong with having strong beliefs outside of the core area I mentioned; as long as those beliefs do not cause contention or disunity in the body. Yes, you may feel strongly about some of them, but does that mean you are absolutely right? Think of how many times in your life you have been so sure, so positive about something you thought was true, and later found yourself to be wrong. The older I get, the more this happens to me. I realize now that I should have a more humble attitude about some things I believe, and always keep an open mind that maybe, just maybe, I could be wrong. As I said before, if great minds in church history disagree on this matter, perhaps I'm not absolutely clear.

Romans and Freedom

Probably the most important text regarding division among
Christians is found in Romans 14. The text is so liberating that I
refer to it often, especially when discussing my ministry, Fans for
Christ.

Fans for Christ is a Christian group for a certain type of,
dare I say it: freaks. We are fans of science fiction, fantasy, all
kinds of games, renaissance fairs, Japanese animation, and many
other interests that bring fans together. Our purpose is fairly
simple. We want to provide a community for Christians who enjoy
these fan interests, and also reach out to those who don't
understand both sides of our lives. We try to reach out to
Christians to show them that what we do is not wrong, not sin, and
certainly not of "the devil." Some Christians maintain that if you
read books or play games with any reference to "magic" that you
are involved in the occult. However, the "magic" in Harry Potter,
or Lord of the Rings, or the Chronicles of Narnia is based on
fantasy, not reality. It is simply a creation of the imagination. It is a
story, and stories often have morals and lessons. They have good
and evil. How can you have the good guys win if there is no bad
guy? Yet some critics would warn against watching Star Wars lest
you be tempted by "the Dark Side." These entertainments are
movies and books, not manuals for a religion or philosophies of
living. Many of these are fun and good and God is pleased when
we enjoy ourselves.

Earlier I mentioned speaking to a Christian counselor about
my anxiety and showed you the diagram he gave me. He also said
to me that God is a God of joy. If we look to the feasts of the Old
Testament, we see a nation with week long celebrations endorsed
by God! Deuteronomy says about the feast of first fruits that, "you
and the Levites and the aliens among you shall rejoice in all the
good things the LORD your God has given to you and your
household." (26:11) Yes, there were sacrifices and ceremonies for
God, but the rest of the time do you know what the Jews were
doing? Partying and rejoicing! God is pleased to give us the
kingdom, his Son, and all things! (Romans 8:32) I had been so
worried that God was only concerned about me checking off all the

boxes of the right things to do that I had no joy at all in life. Now I am free to enjoy the things I like, in moderation of course. I have been set free by knowing God and his freedom. I now can accept myself when I wear my spikes and my black eyeliner and dress like a Goth, and when I enjoy dressing up as a Gypsy for a renaissance fair, or when I play a game on my Xbox with "magic" in it. Some people like football, but I like this stuff, and it is okay. I don't need to be fixed, or changed. In fact, I celebrate who I am and hope to reach out to other people who are different, who are freaks like me. I want them to know God. That is the other part of Fans for Christ's purpose: to reach out to the fans that don't know God. Many of these people who dress up in costumes for conventions don't have a very good opinion of Christians. They feel like most Christians would find something wrong with them or their lifestyle. We want to show them that there are at least some of us who understand, who call ourselves Christians yet are fans like them. Then maybe they will finally realize that they could be a Christian too, that they could be accepted by God for who they are.

This brings me to the book of Romans, Chapter 14. Let's take a look at it.

Romans 14: The Weak and the Strong

 Accept him whose faith is weak, without passing judgment on disputable matters. One man's faith allows him to eat everything, but another man, whose faith is weak, eats only vegetables. The man who eats everything must not look down on him who does not, and the man who does not eat everything must not condemn the man who does, for God has accepted him. Who are you to judge someone else's servant? To his own master he stands or falls. And he will stand, for the Lord is able to make him stand.

 One man considers one day more sacred than another; another man considers every day alike. Each one should be fully convinced in his own mind. He who regards one day as special, does so to the Lord. He who eats meat, eats to the Lord, for he gives thanks to God; and he who abstains, does so to the Lord and gives thanks to God. For none of us lives to himself alone and none of us dies to himself alone. If we live, we live to the Lord; and if we die, we die to the Lord. So, whether we live or die, we belong to the Lord.

For this very reason, Christ died and returned to life so that he might be the Lord of both the dead and the living. You, then, why do you judge your brother? Or why do you look down on your brother? For we will all stand before God's judgment seat. It is written:
" 'As surely as I live,' says the Lord,
'every knee will bow before me;
every tongue will confess to God.' " So then, each of us will give an account of himself to God.

Therefore let us stop passing judgment on one another. Instead, make up your mind not to put any stumbling block or obstacle in your brother's way. As one who is in the Lord Jesus, I am fully convinced that no food is unclean in itself. But if anyone regards something as unclean, then for him it is unclean. If your brother is distressed because of what you eat, you are no longer acting in love. Do not by your eating destroy your brother for whom Christ died. Do not allow what you consider good to be spoken of as evil. For the kingdom of God is not a matter of eating and drinking, but of righteousness, peace and joy in the Holy Spirit, because anyone who serves Christ in this way is pleasing to God and approved by men.

Let us therefore make every effort to do what leads to peace and to mutual edification. Do not destroy the work of God for the sake of food. All food is clean, but it is wrong for a man to eat anything that

causes someone else to stumble. It is better not to
eat meat or drink wine or to do anything else that
will cause your brother to fall.

So whatever you believe about these things keep
between yourself and God. Blessed is the man who
does not condemn himself by what he approves. But
the man who has doubts is condemned if he eats,
because his eating is not from faith; and everything
that does not come from faith is sin.

There are many, many issues that can fit into this category. Here
Paul uses the example of food, and also about what days are holy.
What are we called to do if we disagree? We are not to judge, not
to look down on our brother, and also to keep it between ourselves
and God. Can you imagine a church where people kept these kinds
of things between God and themselves? All of those people who
feel it is their job to go around correcting everyone, making sure
they believe their way, the "right" way, would instead… shut up
and love everyone.

Do not destroy the work of God for the sake of food, Paul
says. If someone is in the church with you and they believe in
Jesus, *they are saved.* They are going to be with God forever, just
like you and *you don't need to save them again.* They don't need to
be saved from dating, or from their premillenialism, or from infant
baptism, or from whatever strong personal belief you happen to
think is wrong. See, they have God to talk to about that stuff. As
Christians we are in relationship with God. The work is done
already when someone is born by the Spirit into God's kingdom.
Yes, we should grow as Christians together, but don't make a
secondary issue as important as the gospel. Don't make it so
important it separates you from your brothers and sisters, so you
judge them and look down on them.

The chapter above tells us that we will answer to God. We
do not have to put up every bit of our lives up for scrutiny by every
other Christian. Yet, the fact that we will answer to God should
make us humble and watch what we do. We should fear God, not
man. We answer to God, and God alone. At the final judgment,
when the books are opened, William from Thursday night Bible

study is not going to be the one up there making the decisions – God will be. So, if you are consumed by fear about what others in your church or group think of you, I pray you will be released by this chapter. If you are the one looking down on others for not being "right" (by not agreeing with you) then I pray you instead see your brothers and sisters through God's eyes and love them despite their differences. They have more need of your love than your judgment.

Paul acknowledges that there are, indeed, disputable matters. Right there in the Bible. There are matters that are not perfectly clear. Why? Because again, the Bible is not meant to be a rulebook, it is the story of God and us, and his plan of salvation. It reveals to us who God is and how he loves us, not the list of things we have to do to make God happy. So there are matters that aren't always clear. We can accept that and live. We don't always have to have all the answers. Yet we can try to always love our brothers and sisters. Remember back to the chapter on people being different – if you don't know someone that well, they may have gone through some terrible experiences, things that shape how they think. Getting to know them and understanding them will be much more beneficial to them than preaching to them about your personal belief system.

People often reference Romans 14, but it is more often used to tell others what to do, sadly, by using the excuse to not cause someone else to stumble. Certainly, there are things we can do to tempt our brothers and sisters, yet living a life of freedom in Christ doesn't mean you are always stumbling others. If there is something you do that bothers a brother or sister, it doesn't mean you have to stop doing it, just stop doing it *around them*. Keep it to yourself, like the verse says above. Yet, don't let people use this verse to take away your freedom and tell you what to do. Looking out for another Christian is an act of love, let it remain that.

Love First, Everything Else Second

Jesus said, "A new command I give you: Love one another. As I have loved you, so you must love one another. **By this all men will know that you are my disciples, if you love one another.**" (John 13:34-35) Love is was so important, so defining, that Jesus said that is how people will know we are Christians. He didn't say they will know us by how we dress, or how we don't ever say a swear word, or by our acting all holy, or even by our memorizing the entire Bible. He said they will know and recognize us by our love. Jesus prayed for us to be one, as we read in John 17. You may have heard the old hymn that was written based on this verse:

We are one in the Spirit, we are one in the Lord
We are one in the Spirit, we are one in the Lord
And we pray that all unity may one day be restored
And they'll know we are Christians by our love, by our love
They will know we are Christians by our love

I pray that we will learn to love first and foremost as Christians. That we will learn to see beyond our own cultural preferences and secondary beliefs to the individual person that God loves. That we will no longer feel that everyone else has to be "like us" to be good, or right, or a "real" Christian. How important is this love? Let us let the Bible tell us.

> If I speak in the tongues of men and of angels, but have not love, I am only a resounding gong or a clanging cymbal. If I have the gift of prophecy and can fathom all mysteries and all knowledge, and if I have a faith that can move mountains, but have not love, I am nothing. If I give all I possess to the poor and surrender my body to the flames, but have not love, I gain nothing. – I Cor 13:1-3

We can have amazing faith, spiritual gifts, understand all the knowledge, and give everything to the poor and be **nothing** without love. All those things above are not bad things, but without love they are useless. So love is, therefore, first and foremost to be desired. More than knowledge, more than spiritual gifts, more than service. In love we are humble toward each other. Yet knowledge without love tends to make us feel superior to others. Paul also says in I Corinthians, "We know that we all possess knowledge. Knowledge puffs up, but love builds up. The man who thinks he knows something does not yet know as he ought to know. But the man who loves God is known by God."

Love is what brings us closer to God. Love is what God himself is, as the book of I John tells us, "God is love." Knowledge, without love, only puffs us up. It makes us think more of ourselves than we should. It can make us think we know things we don't. But love builds up. It encourages, trusts, protects. If we use our knowledge with love, then we will build others up. Yet we must remember, always, that love is more important than the knowledge. Without love, knowledge is nothing, as Paul said above. With love, the knowledge can be used properly to help others, for their good. Without love, knowledge can be a discouragement, a condemnation, even something that pushes someone away from God. I used to want to have all the answers, but now I want to learn how to really love.

Intellectualism and Western Thought

It seems a very common part of the Western mindset to want to break everything down to logic, even faith -- which really is beyond logic. Before we talked about our desire to "understand everything" which I believe can become an idol. We have taken the Bible and tried to force it into the mold of Westernized thinking and logic. We want everything in there to make "logical sense." In fact if it doesn't, we get disturbed and it bothers us. Yet this is something that Westerners, including us Americans, have decided upon; we want *everything* to be perfectly logical and explainable. We feel like we must have *all* the answers so if anyone questions our Christianity we can give them a clear answer. For everything.

Yet this may represent a lack of faith. What brings people to God? Is it our amazing understanding of the Bible and apologetics and reason? Or is it the Spirit of God Himself that draws people to him and regenerates them? The words of God and the message of the gospel are what have the power, not our powers of reason and intellect. Do we not have faith in the power of the Gospel? Do we feel like if we have any logical "holes" in our beliefs that God's power will not be in our personal witness? If we do, we should think about where our faith lies. We are simply the bearers of a message that transcends mere logic. God's power is what saves, not our power.

I read in Neil Cole's book *The Organic Church* about a missionary who had years of experience and traveled the world. He knew his apologetics, his reason and logic for believing in God. This missionary was speaking to a Satanist about Jesus. The missionary asked him what he did with the person of Jesus, and the Satanist actually said he thought a lot of what Jesus said was good. So the missionary brought out the argument that because Jesus claimed to be God, he was either the Lord, a Liar, or a Lunatic. Before he got halfway through his argument the Satanist basically said, "Yes, that is from C.S. Lewis, I have read his books and enjoy them, thanks." He then ended the conversation. Later Neil tells of that same Satanist talking to a new believer. This girl, he fears, doesn't know that much about the Bible yet, and perhaps the Satanist will blow her faith away. Instead, when she talks to him she says, "For many years I would go to bed at night and wonder if anyone in the whole universe cared if I would wake up the next day or not. Then I met Jesus, and I don't go to bed lonely anymore. I know that Jesus loves me and he cares about what is going on in my life." Her message reached the young Satanist more than any logic did. Why? Because it contained the power of God spoken from the heart.

Eastern philosophy and belief has many facets, and one of them involves accepting what to us is a logical paradox. Have you heard of the "sound of one hand clapping"? We seek to eliminate paradox; yet the Eastern mindset was to embrace it.

I think we run into trouble because there are some things in the Bible that are just beyond our understanding; at least in a logical sense. God says that to us that his ways and thoughts are not our ways and thoughts. (Isa 55:8) So, why do we seek to take everything in the Bible and force it to make logical, rational sense? God himself says that he is so far above us we cannot comprehend him. There is mystery in that – there is beauty.

I am glad that God left us with some mystery; for instance, the Trinity. We can make analogies for it, try to explain it, yet the concept of the three who are one still is a bit of a paradox to us. And that's *not a bad thing*. The point is that there are parts of the Bible that encourage what may seem to be different points of view.

Yes, they seem to conflict, but that is only using our frail human logic. In God's eyes it all makes sense, but why must we insist that it make sense to us? Why not view it a divine mystery that God has given us? Can't we see it as something beyond our comprehension? Has our arrogance to know and understand everything made us blind to the beauty of mystery?

We should be okay with not understanding certain things. We don't have to know it all and put it all in little compartments and boxes of logic. Once we are able to let go in this area our faith can be more of an experience with God and less of an intellectual exercise. We will, instead of turning to logic to understand the Bible, turn to the Spirit of God to teach us and help us. We can come to the point where we can say, I do not know why God made things this way, but I do know that *they are this way.*

Remember the verse about knowledge puffing up? When we get puffed up by our knowledge, it can divide us because we will look down on others who disagree with what our reason and logic tells us. Yet, no one has said that God must follow our Western idea of logic. There are, in God, qualities that are beyond just Eastern or Western thinking. To limit our perspective of God to our Western culture limits who he is and can be. His ways really are amazingly above ours. We cannot comprehend an infinite God's wisdom. Remember what seems foolishness to the world is wisdom to God. I have known too many people whose faith and experience with God is purely intellectual. They do not feel his presence, know his power, or experience his revelation through the Spirit. It is all books, and reason, and dry logic with them. That is not our God, our God is *alive* and lives in us!

Unity in the Body

Jesus prayed for our unity. The Bible authors under inspiration of the Spirit wrote about how wonderful unity is, and how as Christians we should be united together as one. We have a picture of oneness in the Bible in marriage. A picture of two people becoming "one flesh," as it is referred to. Marriage is a representation of being one with God. Yes, as intimate as we are physically with our mate, God wants us to be with him spiritually. So close that we will be called *one.*

In Psalms, unity is praised:

Psalm 133

How good and pleasant it is
    when brothers live together in unity!
It is like precious oil poured on the head,
    running down on the beard,
    running down on Aaron's beard,
    down upon the collar of his robes.
It is as if the dew of Hermon
    were falling on Mount Zion.
    For there the LORD bestows his blessing,
    even life forevermore.

Now, I don't really know how good it was when oil poured down unto Aaron's beard, but the author makes it sound pretty darn good. Precious and beautiful even. The theme of unity is all over the New Testament.

Ephesians 4:3 "Make every effort to keep the unity of the Spirit through the bond of peace."

Ephesians 4:12-13 "so that the body of Christ may be built up until we all reach unity in the faith and in the knowledge of the Son of God"

I Corinthians 1:10 "I appeal to you, brothers, in the name of our Lord Jesus Christ, that all of you agree with one another so that there may be no divisions among you and that you may be perfectly united in mind and thought."

One of the most important concepts of unity is that the church is the Body of Christ. Not "a" body of Christ, but THE Body of Christ. There can be only one.

Therefore, as God's chosen people, holy and dearly loved, clothe yourselves with compassion, kindness,

humility, gentleness and patience. Bear with each
other and forgive whatever grievances you may
have against one another. Forgive as the Lord
forgave you. And over all these virtues put on love,
which binds them all together in perfect unity. Let
the peace of Christ rule in your hearts, since as
members of one body you were called to peace. --
Colossians 3: 12-15

Paul talks about the church as one body often, in I Corinthians 12
he talks about how we each have different gifts and serve different
purposes in the body.

The body is a unit, though it is made up of many
parts; and though all its parts are many, they form
one body. So it is with Christ. For we were all
baptized by one Spirit into one body—whether Jews
or Greeks, slave or free—and we were all given the
one Spirit to drink. (v 12-13)

No matter where we came from or who we are, as believers we are
one in the body of Christ. In I Corinthians 12 we often read it in
the context of individuals each being a part of the body. That is
true, but think about this: the actual body of Christ, which is made
up of all believers, is *huge*. It is bigger than just one church
membership. It is *all* of the faithful of God. We may usually think
of being part of the body as having a role in our local church – but
let us expand the scope to the full body of Christ. Not just your
local church, not just the ones in your country or your continent –
but the *whole world.* In that context, the Baptists are one part of the
body. The Methodists are another, and so for each denomination.
So then, let us consider as Paul continues in Corinthians:

Now the body is not made up of one part but of
many. If the foot should say, "Because I am not a
hand, I do not belong to the body," it would not for
that reason cease to be part of the body. And if the
ear should say, "Because I am not an eye, I do not
belong to the body," it would not for that reason

cease to be part of the body. If the whole body were
an eye, where would the sense of hearing be? If the
whole body were an ear, where would the sense of
smell be? But in fact God has arranged the parts in
the body, every one of them, just as he wanted them
to be. If they were all one part, where would the
body be? As it is, there are many parts, but one
body. (v 14-20)

It is good that there are diverse kinds of churches and styles of
worship. It is good that we can find a place to worship that better
meets our Spiritual needs. Yet the way the Church is meant to exist
is as **one body.** Surely, each part can do its own individual job, but
unless *all of the parts work together* they are not functioning as a
body. What does this mean? It means that all of us Christians out
there who hold to the truth of the gospel should be together and not
separate. There are times when we should function as a body, and
not as a part of one.

We should think of ourselves as Christians first, and our
denomination second, as I have said. We should see ministries and
outreaches and missions that are a joint effort between
denominations. And we do see that. My heart has been encouraged
that in the last decade I have seen new ministries appear. Ministries
that bring together Christians from different denominations to
work together – even Catholics and Protestants. That is a
wonderful thing. Yet it is sad that there are so many types of
Christians that not only separate themselves from each other, but
despise each other or say that the others are from the devil himself!

There are so many gaps it is impossible to mention them all
but I want to name a few, call them out, as it were, to unity.
Certain evangelicals think that charismatics – those that believe
that the gifts of the Spirit are meant for today – are actually getting
in touch with the Devil. This is based on one scripture that implies
that maybe the gifts of the Spirit mentioned in the Bible may have
ceased, but it is by no means perfectly clear. (I Cor 13:8) This
verse is even in the middle of the "love chapter" in the Bible! Yet
it seems that there is little love for those who might, dare I say it,
speak in "tongues" occasionally. Can it be that someone genuinely
seeking after God and the spiritual gifts is pursuing the devil? In

the next chapter of I Corinthians, Paul tells those in his letter to "eagerly desire spiritual gifts." So those that pursue them also believe they are following the Bible. Sometimes Charismatics will look down on those without the gifts as "second class" Christians as well. Should we destroy the kingdom of God over this dispute? Should we call our brothers "of the devil?" I pray that if you are on either side of this you will allow for grace in this matter, and pursue unity and love as God desires.

Yes, Protestants and Catholics disagree on some major issues, but does that mean that members of each should automatically assume that the others are not saved? How do you know someone's personal relationship with God? Can you look at someone and tell if they have received salvation? Each of us should deal with people as individuals, and not write off an entire group of people as the same. We are all different. There are good and bad Protestants and Catholics, by name. The *Christians* are the ones who call upon Jesus for their salvation and know him as their God, and being a Catholic or Protestant is second to being a Christian.

Some churches think that worship should be very methodical and reverent, and others that it should be a celebration with clapping and dancing. There are times for both, even in the Bible. Why should one look down on the other? Don't we all call on the name of Jesus as our God? I don't have room to list all of the conflicts; it would take an entire book! Yet consider this: should we let women pastors, or infant baptism, or eschatology, or predestination or any other issue separate us? We are one body!

We have seen that we can be right about *everything* but if we do not love we are *nothing*. God desires us to be one body, to be one in unity. Love is the key to it all. Knowledge will puff us up, but love will build up. If we love each other first and foremost as we are supposed to, we will truly become one – something Jesus and Paul both prayed for.

> May they be brought to complete unity to let the
> world know that you sent me and have loved them
> even as you have loved me. -- John 17:23

He prayed for complete unity so that the world would know God sent him! Jesus also told us that they will know us by our love. The world then, will know Christians by our love and our unity. How far short have we fallen from this goal when we let divisions come up among us? How powerful is the body when it is fighting against itself? There are disorders of the human body where it attacks itself – autoimmune disorders. One of the chief types of this disorder is Multiple Sclerosis. With no offense to those who have the condition, the Church today is suffering from a huge case of MS! We attack our own body. Can we be healthy in this condition? No, we are weak, divided against ourselves. What is the cure? Love.

Love is shown as the most desirable trait of a Christian, it is the way we should appear to the world, it is in the two most important commandments and God himself is love. We should, in love, hold true to the core message of the gospel and, in love, be in unity with those others who call upon the name of Jesus as their savior. If we are able to accept differences within the body of Christ, then we will be more open to different types of people in the body of Christ. We won't try to change them or say you can't be "X" and also be a Christian. We will then be open to different people being Christians, will be open to the people we look at as freaks and instead see them as our brothers and sisters. In love we can learn that not all Christians have to be exactly the same as us, and don't have to agree with us on every issue. We can learn to treat each person as an individual, with their own problems and history, and not box them into our black and white rules. It is this love that thinks of *others* first, and then itself. It loves first and foremost, instead of judging. I can't say it better than God does himself in his word:

> Love is patient, love is kind. It does not envy, it
> does not boast, it is not proud. It is not rude, it is not
> self-seeking, it is not easily angered, it keeps no
> record of wrongs. Love does not delight in evil but
> rejoices with the truth. It always protects, always
> trusts, always hopes, always perseveres.
> Love never fails. -- I Cor 13:4-8

Chapter 7

God Looks at the Heart

People are often very concerned with their outward appearance. We go through our day, conscious of how we appear to other people. When people come to visit our houses or apartments, we apologize for the mess. We don't want people to think we are normally that messy. We check our smile in the bathroom after eating a salad to make sure there isn't a half of a lettuce leaf sticking between our teeth. Appearance does affect how we live our lives in this world; there is no doubt about it.

As I have admitted before, I am a gothic type of person. I usually dress in black and spiked bracelets. Well, recently I was shopping for a car. I called some people to test drive their cars they had for sale. Before I left the house, I made a decision to dress like a *normal person.* I didn't wear my spiked bracelets or all black; I put on jean shorts, tennis shoes (which I had to dig out of my closet from underneath the boots) and a t-shirt. I was... *normal boy.* "Hello there sir, wouldn't you like to sell me your car? I'm perfectly normal!"

I knew that some people would react negatively to me in my usual clothes and accessories (not to mention the eyeliner.) If they viewed me negatively, they might not give me as good of a deal on the car. The negotiations could start off with things unfavorable in my direction. I figured this was important enough to set aside my fashion, just for a day, and try to get a better deal for myself on the car. Well, I went and test drove a couple of cars, and the people were very nice and polite. I don't know what would have happened if I had dressed the way I usually do because I don't really know them, but I felt it still was to my advantage. Probably it would be even more to my advantage if I wore a tie, who knows?

The fact is, these people didn't know me but they probably made a lot of decisions about me by how I was dressed. It is just part of how we do things. Yet it is not the way God does things.

In I Samuel 16, Saul has been rejected by God as Israel's king. Samuel, his prophet, is called to anoint a new king that God has chosen. God has told him that this king is one of the sons of Jesse of Bethlehem. So, Samuel goes to Jesse's house. Right away he sees Jesse's son Eliab, and thinks that he must be the new king.

> When they arrived, Samuel saw Eliab and thought, "Surely the LORD's anointed stands here before the LORD." But the LORD said to Samuel, "Do not consider his appearance or his height, for I have rejected him. The LORD does not look at the things man looks at. Man looks at the outward appearance, but the LORD looks at the heart." -- I Samuel 16:6-7

Man does look at the outward appearance, yes. God knew who would make the best king, and it wasn't necessarily a man who was tall or large and strong. It was a man whose heart was able to lead Israel. In Acts, David is called a man after God's own heart. (Acts 13:22) This is what was important; what was inside David. Not how he looked, because he was not a large man. You probably know that David was a small man. But that didn't matter to God, it was David's heart he looked at.

This is just another example of how God's ways are not the ways of the world. Yet somehow we let this world influence us as Christians. In many churches, there are standards for appearance. Now, it is all well and good to be moral and cover up your naughty parts, but that's not what I'm talking about. One church I was in questioned you if you were male and you wore an earring. They never came right out and said it, but if you wore one, there was the implication that somehow, it was a sin.

Somehow churches have overemphasized appearance. This is another area where Jesus condemned the Pharisees. He was invited to have a meal at the house of a Pharisee, and this is what happened

> When Jesus had finished speaking, a Pharisee invited him to eat with him; so he went in and reclined at the table. But the Pharisee, noticing that Jesus did not first wash before the meal, was surprised. – Luke 11:37-38

Think about this: do you really believe that Jesus did not know that the Jews always washed their hands before eating, and merely forgot? No, Jesus broke this "tradition" on purpose. Why did he do that? Well, let us look at what happens next.

> Then the Lord said to him, "Now then, you
> Pharisees clean the outside of the cup and dish, but
> inside you are full of greed and wickedness. You
> foolish people! Did not the one who made the
> outside make the inside also? But give what is
> inside the dish to the poor, and everything will be
> clean for you. – Luke 11:39-41

To God, it doesn't really matter how nice or pretty or saintly or sacrificing we seem on the outside. It matters what is really in our heart. Somehow in the church, we have equated putting up an appearance with the witness of the Holy Spirit. People say things like, "Well, I don't want to damage my witness by…" And follow that with things like: wearing an earring, smoking, having a tattoo, dressing differently than the church style.

Our faith on people coming to God through us seems to have nothing to do with God, and everything to do with our appearance! Yet, it is God who saves, God who draws others to him. Jesus said that, "No one can come to me unless the Father who sent me draws him." (John 6:44) Shouldn't our faith be that God draws people to him? Now Jesus did say to preach the gospel and tell others, so we are to be a witness. But how? By being a Pharisee and being all holy and saintly looking on the outside? By the fact that we never say a curse word and make a face when someone else around us does?

In the last Chapter we saw that Jesus said people would know we are Christians by our love. *So many times* I hear people talk about how their *moral living* is what will make people see that they are different from others. They say, "I want people to see what makes Christians different from the rest of the world. I want them to look at me and go, 'Wow, they have something different.'" They might indeed do that, but what they think probably won't be,

"Wow, I wish I could have that! I wish I could be so nice and good and moral like them!"

People aren't out in the world dying in their need to be moral. They are dying in their need for *forgiveness.* Grace is what makes the gospel message unique. As Christians, we don't magically turn into superhuman beings that no longer sin. Remember the old bumper sticker, "Not perfect, just *forgiven.*" We aren't perfect and we shouldn't try to convince the world that we are just because we are Christians. Our witness should be in our love for others, not our desire to show off our morality. What people are dying for, starving for spiritually, is the knowledge that God is ready to forgive and love them *just the way they are right now.* He stands there saying, "Come to me and I will give you rest."

I recently got to interview a Christian sci-fi actress, Brandy Ledford. She played the android, Doyle, on the sci-fi series *Andromeda.* During the interview, I asked her what challenges and difficulties she faced being a Christian in the Hollywood scene. She said, "Oh, it's actually easier now." I was in momentary shock. Easier? With all of Hollywood's animosity toward Christianity? With the world pressuring her to take off her clothes and do other things that are worldly? "Oh, I turn down those parts," she said. "It is easier now because the shame is gone. I am forgiven. All those things in my past don't weigh me down anymore."

I met Brandy at one of the biggest sci-fi and fantasy conventions in the country: DragonCon. She saw our table for Fans for Christ there and came up to talk to us. She was very glad there was someone reaching out to the fan community, and she told us how she was a Christian. She accepted one of our Fans for Christ badges, and even wore it at the table where she was signing autographs. During our conversation she said she was happy to use her notoriety as a way to tell people about Jesus. At that convention, if you were dressed *normally* you would have stood out. People in costume from fantasy and sci-fi and comic books and you name it were wandering around; over 20,000 of them. Probably some of these people think they would have to give up their costumes and their unique style of dressing to be a Christian. My group, Fans for Christ, hopes to change that. We want to show them that what God really cares about is your heart, not what you wear or what fashion you like.

What Really Attracts People

So many people talk about how you can't be a Christian and be "worldly." But what does that mean? We are told to be in the world but not "of" the world. Then we shouldn't just separate ourselves completely and live on a compound with all the other Christians. We are to be out there, with others, showing them the light. Yet, the Bible calls us a separate, holy people. What makes us separate? In I Corinthians 6 Paul is exhorting Christians to live holy lives, and he says, "But you were washed, you were sanctified, you were justified in the name of the Lord Jesus Christ and by the Spirit of our God." *Sanctified* means to be set apart for holy use. We are God's and are his to use. Yet we must remember what makes us holy is the blood of Jesus, the Savior, the Redeemer, the Messiah. It is not what we do. What we have that makes us separate is *Jesus.* We try to live a good life because we follow Jesus, we love Jesus, and we want to honor him. Not because we can earn Jesus, or prove he exists, or impress others. Our own efforts will fail us, but as followers of Christ, even in our mistakes we will point to the grace of God and his Son.

We can put the cart before the horse, and try to be holy and good so we can show off our Christianity and look good and maybe try to impress God or people with our behavior. Yet the Bible says no matter how good we act, how moral we are, we are still filthy, our own righteousness is filled with ugly sin in God's eyes. (Romans 3:10) When we are correct in understanding our own sin and our inability to truly be good on our own, then we become humble. Then we become more forgiving of other's faults. We stop looking at the outward appearance of others because we know in the inside, our own hearts are sick, needing the cure of Jesus.

This is what I think. I think that what will astonish and amaze people is our God-given ability, through the Holy Spirit, to *love others*. Jesus said in Matthew 5, "I tell you: Love your enemies." Love our *enemies*? How crazy is that? I tell you what, the world does not do it neither can it comprehend it. Jesus continues and says, "If you love those who love you, what reward will you get? Are not even the tax collectors doing that?" It is *easy* to love others that love you, even the world does that. Everybody does that. You want to seem different? Show them the power of God you have in loving those who hate you, who persecute you, who are your enemy. You can't do this on your own any more than you can do anything else as a Christian, but you have the Spirit and the power and the *love* inside you.

Another thing I think that makes us different from the world, in our *heart*, not on the outside, is our faith. When we know God, we know he will take care of us. We *know* he loves us and promised to take care of us. He even promised that all things will work for our good! (Romans 8:28) How we react to suffering and trials can be an amazing witness to others. While people of the world may curse and cry and moan and despair, we can stand on our faith in God. We can confess that Jesus is our God and loves us and no matter what happens that will never change. We have the promise of an eternal reward in heaven and everlasting joy. So, I ask you, should we be grumpy? How many grumpy Christians do you know? If they are unhappy and sour most of the time, perhaps it is that they really don't understand God's love for them, how much they have been forgiven of, and how wonderful it will be to be with God forever? Rich Mullins who wrote the song "Awesome God" once said,

> I think that of all the diseases in the world, the
> disease that all humankind suffers from, the disease
> that is most devastating to us is not AIDS, it's not
> gluttony, it's not cancer, it's not any of those things.
> It is the disease that comes about because we live in
> ignorance of the wealth of love that God has for us.

Now, I'm not saying it's wrong to be sad; grief is normal and acceptable and even Jesus cried for his friend Lazarus. Yet, once our mourning is over, God will turn our tears to joy! What change should being a Christian have on us? We should show the joy at realizing God has accepted and loves us, and not only that, has promised to take care of us forever.

If we spent the rest of our lives learning how to love our enemies, and trying to comprehend the amazing depth of God's love for us and all he has given us, not a second would be wasted. If we really understood what we had, I think our lives would be transformed in a way that is evident to others in an amazing way. Not so much in what we say, but in how we react to life when it is hard or when people hurt us. Faith and love showing through in the face of adversity is a sign of what God can do. That is what I want my witness to be. Steven Curtis Chapman wrote a song about this called, *The Change,* about the difference in our lives that should happen when we know God. Here's a part of it.

Well I got myself a T-shirt that says what I believe
I got letters on my bracelet to serve as my ID
I got the necklace and the key chain
And almost everything a good Christian needs, yeah
I got the little Bible magnets on my refrigerator door
And a welcome mat to bless you before you walk across my floor
I got a Jesus bumper sticker
And the outline of a fish stuck on my car
And even though this stuff's all well and good, yeah
I cannot help but ask myself--

What about the change
What about the difference
What about the grace
What about forgiveness
What about a life that's showing
I'm undergoing the change, yeah
I'm undergoing the change

So, I ask you... what about the grace? What about forgiveness? How have those things affected your *heart*, the part that God is concerned with? That's where God looks when he sees you, not on your outside. Since God is more concerned with our heart and our inside, shouldn't we be also?

Outside is not the inside

How many times have you heard someone say that a person is "beautiful on the inside"? We all in some way realize that who you are on the inside is more important than the exterior, yet we also recognize that a person's appearance does influence us. Sometimes it is with regret that we realize that we are affected by our perception of someone's exterior. We realize that though someone is not physically beautiful, they are still a valuable person, to the people that love them and to God. Imagine if everyone could see all of your faults and that they had physical consequences. What if everyone was like this, where all of our anger and evil thoughts caused our outside to be deformed and ugly? I dare say we would all be hideous, not one of us would be fit to look at. Yet it shows the truth – we all are sinful in our hearts. (Jer 17:9)

We judge people not only by their looks, but also by the clothes they wear. I believe each person has different reasons for what they wear, and different feelings about what clothing means. For my teaching job, I am supposed to wear a tie. Normally I wouldn't want to wear one, but I actually like wearing a tie for my job. It makes me feel professional and respectable. Now, if I did not act professional and respectable, wearing a tie would hardly help. So it is a combination of the two, how I look and how I act. As I mentioned before, when I was going to buy a car I wanted to give a certain impression. However if I acted like a total jerk, that would not help much toward getting them to sell me their car.

So far this is probably pretty obvious to you. But something else happens that should not happen: people make judgments about others purely on appearance. Many times, these people decide they know all they need to know about someone just by looking at them. The sad part is that the person's actions are not considered after this first impression. As Christians I think we tend to do this often. We are so used to seeing "Christians" at church always dressing a certain way. Even at social gatherings we seem to have a "way" of dressing that is somehow "the Christian way."

Now don't get me wrong, of course we should be modest in what we wear. Having said that, just remember that your idea of what is modest may not be someone else's. Modesty can mean a few different things, but here I am simply talking about covering one's nakedness. So, we shouldn't be walking around naked, ok? Now that that's settled, on to bigger issues.

I met a very sweet Christian girl at an anime convention once. She loved to make costumes and loved watching anime. We got to talking, and I came to visit her after the convention a few times. I met her parents and her brothers. We got along extremely well, had lots of fun together, and both shared a strong faith in God. She was living with her parents while attending college. Soon she started to tell me how her parents had doubts about me. Even her brother said, "Nice guys don't drive cars like that." (I have a sports car with dragons on it, I *like* dragons.) Her mother was not happy that I had been divorced. She also said, "Well, he doesn't *look* like a computer teacher." When I was at their house I strived to be as polite and friendly as possible. I said grace over the dinner we shared, and I made sure to thank them for the meal. Their daughter and I were really getting along well and having fun. I thought maybe I had finally found someone like me I could be with. Then I got the email; her parents said she could not see me anymore. She didn't want to go against them because they were paying for her college and she lived with them, even though she was 22 years old. What reason did they give? Nothing I did was cause for concern as far as I remember. It was the car I drove, how I dressed, because I was divorced. I was judged not for who I was, but for external things that had little to do with me. So, I talked with this sweet girl over email a while longer, but then it was over. I know I'm not perfect, but I also know I would have been very good to this nice young lady that I met.

There are lots of reasons people dress the way they do, and it may not be the reasons you think. I am a bit gothic, as I have said, in my style and dress. It means I like to wear black a lot, sometimes some eyeliner, and other accessories. It doesn't mean I worship the devil or I want to be a woman or I am a sociopath. For me, I happen to feel *comfortable* dressing that way. It feels like, well, *me*. I'm not trying to grab people's attention with my differences, and I'm not trying to scare or bother old ladies. I'm just expressing myself and being creative. Like my car; I actually designed the dragon logo on my hood myself and cut it out of the vinyl stripe with an Exacto knife one night. (Boy were my eyes red after that tedious work!) Some people are artists, or just creative and like to express that through their style of clothes. For work I wear what is appropriate; I'm not married to a style. I think that is important. I don't *have* to dress a certain way but I *like* to.

Many people dress in certain styles because it feels like an expression of themselves. Some do because their family or culture dresses that way. Some, because their family or culture *doesn't* dress that way. The thing is, there are so many reasons people have that we can't decide on a person just from their clothes. I know that all black and makeup one someone may look scary to some people but that is not the goal of most people in the Goth subculture. It simply represents a preference. (See the appendix for more on Goth and other cultures.) Remember before I described a church where everyone dressed and talked the same. My vision is a church where we have all kinds of people with different interests and different ways of expressing themselves coming *together* around Jesus Christ and not focusing on outward appearances. If you see someone in a tie-dye shirt and dreadlocks, do you just *assume* that they do drugs? Do you assume that someone who dresses like a rapper is a murderous gang member? More importantly, do we exclude or avoid those simply because they dress differently?

I want to challenge you to go and meet and talk to people that you have avoided in the past simply because of appearance. Yes, some people fit the stereotypes and they exist for a reason. But many people do not. We are all unique. Go and talk to someone you normally would avoid based on appearance and see who they really are. You will find a person with cares and concerns just like yourself. We all need to worry about our cars and what we will eat and our health and the weather and, as the saying goes, we all put our pants on one leg at a time. You would be surprised at what you learn if you just give them a chance. I don't mean just walk up expecting to be repulsed and walk away smugly – they will be able to sense that attitude. Go and really give them a chance. Look at the inside person, not the outside.

If we would do this more, there would be more people in the church. Some people might be upset because the new people coming to church would no longer follow the "American Church Dress Code", but more genuine people would be there worshipping God. Isn't that what we say we really want? So, if we really mean

it, we should act on it. It is time for the church to give up all our
American traditions on how we dress and how we speak in our
own language of "churchianity." The church transcends America,
it transcends this decade, this century, and this world. We should
not try to limit God or his people to one culture. Revelation 5:9
speaks about Jesus, "You are worthy to take the scroll and to open
its seals, because you were slain, and with your blood you
purchased men for God from every tribe and language and people
and nation." Every single tribe, language, and nation has people
purchased by the blood of the Lamb. God's church should look
like a diverse, beautiful tapestry of people that follow his son.
Once we let go of our prejudice toward the outward appearance,
we then can see as God sees and look at the heart. Not judging
others, but learning to accept them as we will explore in the next
chapter.

Chapter 8

The Acceptance of God

Perhaps we have trouble accepting differences in others because we do not accept *ourselves*. We see our own faults and failings constantly before us and despair. We are hard on ourselves, and therefore hard on others as well. Yet what peace would we have if we knew that everything, right now, was all just right? That God is in control, and yes there is sin and yes you have faults and yes there is evil in the world but it is still alright.

I admit I struggle with this myself. When I wake up in the morning, many times the pressure of all the bad things that could happen weighs on my shoulders. The potential for me to fail, for others to do me wrong, or for losing something precious in my life holds a grip of ice around my heart. Then, I must stop myself and remember that God is a God of peace. He has offered us rest and said his burden is light. (Matt 11:28-30)

The key to understanding our acceptance by God is fully knowing our own sinfulness. Yes, indeed, I am saying that you must understand how pitiful and wretched you are without God to be able to live in his acceptance. One might think that we would go around being miserable all the time if we really understood this, and that would be true except for one thing: grace. We are forgiven by God, and accepted into his kingdom the day we turn to him. Just the way we are, we are welcomed. We must hold tightly onto the grace we received from Jesus at the day of our salvation. At that point many of us understood we needed him because of our sin, but many Christians lose that perspective and become focused on their performance later in life.

If we really truly see that we are hopelessly sinful without God, and that nothing in and of ourselves can be good or righteous, then we understand the depth of God's grace and forgiveness. What it means is that on our best day we are no better than on our worst day. God loves and accepts us just the same, *every* day. Maybe you are doing better in your life than you were when you are saved, but you are *no more righteous in yourself* then you were

that first day you came to Jesus. You are righteous in the eyes of
God because of what *Jesus* did, not because of anything *you* did.
So in our hopelessly sinful state, we become aware of the huge
vastness of God's grace.

> For all have sinned and fall short of the glory of
> God, and *are justified freely by his grace* through
> the redemption that came by Christ Jesus. - Romans
> 3:23-24

We all are the same, all sinners. In God's eyes, we all fall short. He
doesn't see degrees of failure, he sees us *all* as having fallen short.
Yet we are justified freely by grace. It was entirely God's doing
that saved us, and those who are saved are *all* saved and
completely saved.

    The next time your sinfulness condemns you in your heart,
remember that there is no condemnation for those who are in Jesus
Christ. (Romans 8:1) You can acknowledge your sin, look at it
squarely and say, "That was wrong," but also rejoice that God's
grace is awesome and wonderful and all-encompassing every time.
We may have remorse for our sin and failure, yet we must always
remember through our successes and failures God's love is never
changing. It is always there for us.

> Give thanks to the God of heaven.
> His love endures forever -- Psalm 136:26

    It is hard for our sinful hearts to understand the depth of
God's grace, where a murderer can repent and be forgiven by God.
Yet when we realize we really are no different from that murderer,
then we can understand how God sees things and how God has
accepted both ourselves and that murderer.

> "You have heard that it was said to the people long
> ago, 'Do not murder, and anyone who murders will
> be subject to judgment.' But I tell you that anyone
> who is angry with his brother will be subject to
> judgment. -- Matthew 5:21

Remember last chapter we said that God looks at the heart? Well, God sees the murder in our hearts we have not acted out. He sees the lies and the evil we have thought. Not just our actions will be judged, but our hearts! If not for grace, we should be in total despair! But Jesus reassures us later in Matthew:

> When the disciples heard this, they were greatly astonished and asked, "Who then can be saved?" Jesus looked at them and said, "With man this is impossible, but with God all things are possible." Matthew 19:24-26

We cannot make our hearts pure enough, yet God accepts us and gives us the righteousness of Jesus when we are justified. Knowing the depths of our sin gives us freedom, the freedom of realizing our own effort is never enough for salvation, that the work is already *finished* by Christ and God sees us as whole in his eyes. This is possible only by God, not by anything we can do.

Accepting Others

When we realize the magnitude of both our sinfulness and God's grace, we can embrace God's acceptance of us and learn to accept ourselves. But it also should give us a new perspective on how we view others. We are no better or worse than anyone else. We have been saved by a work of God in our lives, and without that we would be completely lost. No matter that we have good manners, or a nice house, or give to the poor. We would still be nothing without God. So then there is no more boasting or pride in ourselves. (Romans 3:27)

We must realize that without God we are nothing, and have nothing good in ourselves. Then we can look at others with love and mercy, knowing they are just the same as we are. We should know that on our own, we could have done *anything.* Murder, deceit, violence, depravity, we are capable of it all in certain situations.

John Bradford was martyred during the reign of Queen "Bloody" Mary who executed many Protestants by burning them at the stake. He had a reputation of being a very devout Christian and was appointed as a traveling chaplain after studying theology at the University of Cambridge in England. During his imprisonment in the tower of London, he saw some criminals being led off for execution, and he spoke his most famous words: "There but for the grace of God, go I."

In modern English we might say, "If it were not for God's grace, that could be me right there." *I could be a criminal, I could be a murderer*, he was saying. The grace of God is not only there for our salvation but our very existence. If God's grace was not so awesome, he would not tolerate sinners to take one more breath on this earth! It is by God's grace that we are not lost and caught up in all of the evil of the world. So, no matter what someone else has done or said, remember… without God's grace that could have been *you*.

I used to look down on others that did things I thought were wrong or selfish. I still do sometimes, I admit. However, God has taught me a valuable lesson. I have been pushed to the limit of my human endurance and seen myself nearly break. I know now that under certain conditions, I could do terrible things. I might not even be quite in my right mind if I was tortured or starved or put under terrible emotional strain. The thing is, we don't know what has happened in other people's lives to influence them to be who they are and to do what they do. It could very well be that if the same things had happened to us, we would have reacted in *exactly the same way*. This world is evil and many people have had horrible things happen to them. Can you really be their judge without knowing the events that have shaped their lives? Without God's grace, you could be the same or even worse than they are. Since God loved us, we should also love others. (I John 4:11) When we are given grace and forgiveness by God, we should also show it to everyone else. Jesus told a story about a man who did not appreciate how much he had been forgiven.

> Then Peter came to Jesus and asked, "Lord, how many times shall I forgive my brother when he sins against me? Up to seven times?"Jesus answered, "I tell you, not seven times, but seventy-seven times. "Therefore, the kingdom of heaven is like a king who wanted to settle accounts with his servants. As

he began the settlement, a man who owed him a million dollars* was brought to him. Since he was not able to pay, the master ordered that he and his wife and his children and all that he had be sold to repay the debt. "The servant fell on his knees before him. 'Be patient with me,' he begged, 'and I will pay back everything.' The servant's master took pity on him, canceled the debt and let him go. "But when that servant went out, he found one of his fellow servants who owed him a few dollars. He grabbed him and began to choke him. 'Pay back what you owe me!' he demanded. "His fellow servant fell to his knees and begged him, 'Be patient with me, and I will pay you back.' "But he refused. Instead, he went off and had the man thrown into prison until he could pay the debt. When the other servants saw what had happened, they were greatly distressed and went and told their master everything that had happened. "Then the master called the servant in. 'You wicked servant,' he said, 'I canceled all that debt of yours because you begged me to. Shouldn't you have had mercy on your fellow servant just as I had on you?' In anger his master turned him over to the jailers to be tortured, until he should pay back all he owed."This is how my heavenly Father will treat each of you unless you forgive your brother from your heart." Matt 18:21-35 (*Changed to modern dollar amount by the author.)

There is freedom in knowing who we are in relation to God. We can accept ourselves, and accept others with this knowledge. We have been forgiven much, so we can forgive others. We have been given grace, and now we can extend grace to others.

So surely we can look past other's faults. In the last chapter we discussed looking past the appearance to the heart, to who a person really is. When we see their hearts, now, we should not judge them in light of knowing we too are sinful and do wrong things. We should remember our hearts, and our sin, and in that knowledge see that everyone else is human, just like we are.

Chapter 9

YOU are a Freak

Maybe after seeing the title of this chapter you might think, "Well, um, I am a bit odd sometimes but I certainly am not a *freak.*" But I am here to convince you that yes, you are. All I have to do is make you think about yourself. You probably aren't convinced yet, but we will see.

Think back to when you were a kid. Kids do weird things. There was probably something *odd* that you liked to do. Eventually, some grown ups found out about it and told you it was weird and normal kids don't do that and so you stopped. Let me give you an example. When I was learning to write in the first grade, we had this special paper. It had two horizontal lines going across for the top and the bottom of your letter, and a dotted line halfway between those two so you could write lowercase letters. Well, when I got to the end of a line, sometimes I had a little bit of space left; not enough for a whole letter, but enough for half of one. So, I would write *half of the letter* on the end of one line, and then finish *the other half* on the next line. So my teachers would see half of an 'n' on the one line (which I suppose looked something like an 'r') and then the other half on the next (which probably didn't look like much of anything.) Eventually my teacher pointed this out to my parents as a concern. We had a nice talk explaining how that wasn't the 'normal' way you do it. So, I learned to do it the 'right' way. Of course in that case it's probably for the best, especially for you folks reading this book right now.

The thing is, there has been pressure on you since you were a child to be 'normal.' Many of the weird things you did were coaxed or pressured out of you out of others' desire for you to be 'normal.' Not only do adults bring pressure on children but of course there is pressure from other children. You probably remember how kids were teased and mocked by others for any significant difference they had, whether they could help it or not. There were probably many things you wanted to do or say but didn't because of peer pressure. There might have been a TV show or a toy you liked that you would have hated for anyone to find out about because they would have teased you or thought you were *weird.* Through high school probably the same things happened. You didn't want people to know certain things about you because it would cause derision. You would be mocked, or worse, rejected.

During this time, some people realized that they liked being different enough that they didn't care and started being themselves. Of course they were mocked but they ended up forming their own social group among the rejects. It might be that the only difference between the popular 'normal' kids and the rejects is that they decided to embrace their weirdness and the popular kids moved away from it. Not that I blame them, it is nice to be accepted. It might be worth giving up some weird things you like to be popular. And of course, some people are just born more different than others. Yet we all have those odd tendencies, unusual preferences, and times when we feel different.

Imagine if all those odd tendencies you had as a kid were not corrected out of you, but were encouraged instead. Now I don't mean ones that were bad for you, or caused you to get behind in life (like my half letters) but other ones that were harmless. Why, then we would all be a bit more freaky, wouldn't you say? So you have always had those tendencies, somewhere inside you, to be different. In some people they were suppressed more than others. Yet we all have them. We all have the tendency to be weird sometimes.

Even today, you have things you like to do, or wear, or music you listen to, or a game you like, or something that you are not sure most people would understand. You probably keep it to yourself or only let those closest to you know about. Maybe you only like wearing certain kinds of socks and can't stand to wear any others. Or maybe you love eating chocolate and cheese sandwiches. You have to fold your laundry just *so,* or you like to scream off-key to heavy metal in the shower. The point is, we all are freaky, but some of us show it more than others. We all do things that others would consider *weird,* but not everyone wants to show that part of themselves to others.

I want to encourage you to 'accept your inner freak.' Why? Imagine if everyone was more tolerant of differences in life. What if you felt safe to share your oddities, and so did everyone else?

Suddenly it would be much more 'normal' to be *weird!* The world
would offer more variety, people would be more comfortable with
themselves, and there would not be such a stigma attached to being
'different.' So I tell you: proudly wear your freakiness on your
sleeve! Let the world know you are different and it is okay! It may
just be a small thing. You may feel like you are pretty 'normal'
after all. That's okay, I am not biased against you normal folks;
God loves you too!

Remember you are weird

The next time you see someone who seems odd, remember
that you yourself are weird. Remember your quirks and oddities.
This will encourage you to see how you have things in common
with others, instead of dividing you from them.

Once I was at a small sci-fi and fantasy convention near
where I live in North Carolina. In the same hotel was a business
convention for investors. I was wearing a costume; one of my
medieval outfits with some armor. I was standing by the elevator
by myself in costume when the business convention let out for the
night. Many people, mostly middle aged and dressed in business
attire, flooded out of the room and past me. Some of them didn't
look, but most took notice. Some pointed and laughed. Some made
jokes. A few decided to openly mock me. One man in a suit and tie
took out his lighter and walked up to me, flicking it and saying
"Fire! Fire!" I'm not even sure what he meant. Another lady
remarked that, "It's a bit early for Halloween, isn't it honey?"
Later on that evening after some of them had hit they bar they
found me with some friends and came up to me again. One asked if
we realized we were "grown ups." I admit that at this point I got a
bit upset and said a few choice things to that man. After all the
things everyone had said to me, I had kind of had enough.

Why did these people do this? It was almost like being in
high school. They were all together with the other business types,
and probably visiting from out of town, so they probably had a lot
of courage from numbers and from being away from home. Yet
they showed what was really inside them. At this point in life they
still judged others by appearance. They didn't know me and didn't
care to know me. I was weird, I was different, and so they mocked

me – I was an easy target. I found myself wondering if they had taught their kids not to do the very thing they were doing now. If they realized that they too were weird sometimes, and liked certain odd things, maybe they would not have been so disparaging.

But *you* can remember. You can realize you are weird also and accept your strangeness along with others'. Let your acceptance and love for others show as you truly realize who you are.

Christians are Freaks

Let's face it; we are part of a group that claims *a man rose from the dead.* Not only that, but that this man was God himself on earth. While Christianity is quite popular now, it still separates us from the rest of the world. We still sometimes face ridicule because of our faith. There is prejudice and bias against Christians. Some of it, perhaps is because of bad things we as Christians have done, I admit. Yet some of it is simply because we are *different,* that we dare to believe in unpopular things, like not having sex before marriage. We dare to make statements that we should love others, that we should be true to our spouses, and that we should recognize God's son he sent to earth. Not all of this makes us popular, especially in this culture of "Don't tell me what to believe and I won't tell you."

Those in the world find it hard to believe how we can rejoice when bad things happen, because we know God is with us. Or how we avoid the pleasures of this world and do not live in hedonism. We are freaks, to the world. As Christians, we should not split ourselves up into bickering sub-groups. We should realize that as freaks of the world, we need each other! If someone different from you calls on the name of Christ like you do, do not separate yourself from him, call him a brother! It is hard enough to be in this world as a Christian. Imagine how hard it is to *already be weird* and also be a Christian!

Not only would you find yourself isolated from non-Christians for your faith, but also most Christians because you are different. That is the case with Christian freaks. God has made some of us differently, yet we still follow him. When we all realize we are freaks, inside, and that God still loves and accepts us, we will be able to love and accept all of those who call on the name of Jesus – freaks or not. And we also will be able to share the gospel with those people that in the past we avoided or were or afraid of. I believe this is what we are called to, so if I have convinced you of anything at all, come with me to the next chapter and discover how to reach out to these freaks.

Chapter 10

Reaching out to the Freaks

A friend of mine was in the hospital to have her gall bladder removed. While she was recovering, a friend of hers bought her a Harry Potter book to read, since she was stuck in a hospital bed. Upon seeing the book, the nurses (people that were supposed to be there taking *care* of her) made disparaging remarks. They called it a "witch book" and said maybe they should have their own *book burning* right there at the hospital.

Thankfully, my friend is a Christian. Yet, what happened to her makes her feel like she does not want to be around other Christians, if they act like this. And, unfortunately, many do act this way. I remember for many years I was afraid to admit that I played Dungeons and Dragons to my church friends because of all the negative rumors that the church had about it. The thing is, those nurses and other people who are down on things like Harry Potter as "evil" never actually take the time to read the books or research the truth. Most of them hear it from someone, who heard it from someone else, that it is wrong and therefore it must be. That's what "everyone" is saying, and so it is correct. I've read many web sites and articles that *say* Harry Potter and D&D are full of rituals for real occultism, and claim to be knowledgeable of such things. However what they say on these sites has little or no connection to the actual game or the books at all. Of course, if people never *read* Harry Potter or D&D books, they never would know this. Most people will just accept this as the truth; that it really is of the devil.

I remember one time I was on a drive with my aunt Mary Lou who is a devout Christian. She asked me once about me playing Dungeons and Dragons, and wasn't it wrong? Well, I explained that it was just a game. We sit around and make up a character to play; this is a pretend persona in a fictional world. This "character" exists as really a set of numbers on a piece of paper, which represent abilities such as strength, endurance, intelligence, and so on. Then we use the rules of the game to determine what our character can or cannot do. Usually a few of us get together, put on some music, order a pizza and sit around and play the game and also joke around. The image of people dressing up, lighting candles and performing bizarre rituals is completely false. The game involves rolling dice to determine what happens, but so does Monopoly. (For more on this subject, see the Appendix on Christians, Fantasy, and Dungeons and Dragons.) Anyway, she was open-minded and listened and realized it wasn't so bad after all.

So, what is my point here? If you meet someone who does something that formerly you were biased against, why not ask them about it instead? Let them tell you what they are doing and why, not someone else who doesn't know them. Goths may look scary because they wear black and dark makeup, but I have found them to be most interesting and intellectual people. If you assume they are into worshipping the devil because of how they look, you'll never give them a chance. So instead, talk to them and ask them why they are they way they are. You'll get a lot of different responses, because as I have said, everyone is unique.

Most people tend to make friends with people that are similar to themselves, and that is not a bad thing. As Christians, if we really want to learn to reach out to people, we should learn about people that are *different* from us. That way, we can relate to more people when we talk to them about Christ. All you have to do is make an effort to talk to one person that you normally would avoid. That's a start. Just one person. Then after that, try another. Maybe the first one won't go so well, who knows? Remember these people will also be like you were – used to their own kind. You both may have to overcome assumptions about the other. Just talk, and listen. See what happens.

An Army of Freaks

You see, if we have *more* freaks that come into the church, and we *don't* change them into our cookie-cutter style of American Christianity, we will have more freaks that can go out and talk to *other* freaks. Once a goth, or a hippie, or a punk, or a fan gets saved they can go share God with their peers, with those they are comfortable with that feel comfortable around them. Those new believers will then be able to talk to more freaks and thus will begin God's army of freaks.

Perhaps this is a scary thought to you. Yet I believe this is God's will; for Christians to reach out to everyone, regardless of preferences or culture. Jesus spent time with those rejected by society; he reached out to the freaks. The first believers weren't popular or famous or special; they were just those who listened to the message. Jesus went everywhere and spoke to those who would listen, and left those who would not. Maybe some of the freaks would listen if one of their own spoke to them about God, instead of a generic bible thumper in a suit and tie? Can you imagine, all over the country, those who were considered freaks rising up and proclaiming Jesus in their lives? It would appeal to so many people who before never listened. And this could happen, if the church started reaching out to freaks, and stopped trying to change them after they came to Christ.

Those That Have Left

Already I have seen so many people through my ministry say they left church and never went back. Not because they didn't like the church or stopped believing in God, but because they felt they would not be accepted for who they really were. A lot of people like me, who love fantasy stories and Japanese anime and gaming, have left because they felt these interests would be frowned upon. Sadly I have seen it is true, the church is against using your imagination to dream of beautiful places and things and great stories both wonderful and tragic. Yet there is so much beauty in these stories and so much to learn from them. C.S. Lewis knew that when he wrote his books about Narnia.

We are in the midst of a crisis in the church. Those who don't fit our increasingly narrow mold are starting to feel rejected. They feel they would never be accepted, that many interests they have would be rejected as evil or selfish. Somehow it is more accepted to miss church service to watch your favorite football team than to make it to church dressed as a punk. Now of course not all churches are this way and I'm not accusing them all of being narrow minded. Yet there are *so many* people I talk to like me that feel they cannot go to church, cannot belong to the community there. What has happened? Where have we gone wrong? Why is it that we are constantly narrowing the definition of being a Christian? If we keep going it will be so narrow that it will be more like a cult! Everyone will talk, dress, and act the same and speak in Christianese, "Oh hello Jim, I am blessed today! After that exhortation I was convicted and repented!"

I don't believe this is God's vision for the church. There is a reason Paul said he was a Jew to the Jews and a Greek to the Greeks.

> Though I am free and belong to no man, I make myself a slave to everyone, to win as many as possible. To the Jews I became like a Jew, to win the Jews. To those under the law I became like one under the law (though I myself am not under the law), so as to win those under the law. To those not having the law I became like one not having the law (though I am not free from God's law but am under Christ's law), so as to win those not having the law. To the weak I became weak, to win the weak. I have become all things to all men so that by all possible means I might save some. I do all this for the sake of the gospel, that I may share in its blessings. – I Cor 9:19-23

It was so important to Paul to win souls to Christ, he became 'a slave to everyone.' He spoke as a Jew to the Jews, and like a Greek to the Greeks. He became what he could so those around him could be saved. Would Paul be approving of us creating a church culture that excludes people who simply have different tastes and interests, a different *culture?* What he says here in Corinthians is the opposite of that. Yet we are *losing* people from the church because they feel they must *choose between individuality and Jesus.* Some people choose Jesus but are forced to lose who they are, and even worse, some *walk away* from Jesus because of restrictions He would have never imposed. Neither one of these scenarios is acceptable. God made us as beautiful and unique creations, and his church should look that way. No one should feel like they have to become a robot or a cookie-cutter to become a Christian. Certainly, we must follow Jesus and his ways, but we don't have to act and talk like everyone else as robots.

We are encouraged to follow God's commands and love one another, but we are all different people. We have different colors, different interests, different tastes, and different families. We should not seek to make everyone like us; we should instead seek to introduce everyone to our wonderful loving Father and his Son. He loved us first, and now we love him. Our love, the love he has given us, should be given to others.

I pray that if you are a freak, that this message has blessed you and let you know you are accepted and loved by God. If you do not consider yourself one of these outcasts, I pray that your heart be opened to them as individuals, human beings, just like yourself. I pray that there be unity between all those who call on the name of Jesus, and that we see a new harvest begin, the harvest of the freaks. I hope you will be a part of it.

Appendix A: Who are the Goths?

    The Goth subculture has grown since it started in the late 70's and 80's from the punk culture. To understand what it is now, we should first look at where it came from.

    Most of the early goth culture claimed an interest in the dark side of life – horror movies, dark clothing, coffins, the idea of death and sadness. A lot of the music represented this as well. Bauhaus is considered one of the first "goth bands."

    Goth culture centers around an interest in personal style and dress, certain styles of music, the romanticized dark side of life, and a sense of individuality. From the original interests of Goth, the culture grew large enough to eventually spawn its own sub-groups inside it. There are now raver Goths, perky Goths, romantic Goths, cyber-goths, industrial Goths (or rivet heads), and many others. Most of these Goths still center around black dress (though some types use bright colored accents to the black) and the music. Let's take a look at the music, the clothing, and the philosophy of Goths.

So what kind of music do Goths listen to? Goth started frompunk, as I mentioned. The music became a bit darker, about more sad subjects and about death. Influence from the horror movie genre was seen in the lyrics. Eventually other music was identified with the Goth scene, in the 80's many Goths listened to synth-pop, especially The Cure. Modern Goth musical interests include those types of music, but also techno, industrial, and dance music with a heavy bass beat known as EBM. Many Goths enjoy dancing, and have their own style of dance. If you go to a "Goth club", you'll probably see many of the different types of Goths there, some dancing, some talking, and some merely brooding in a corner.

The clothing, as I said, is mainly black. Depending on the Goth's style you may also see leather with spikes, vinyl outfits, fishnets shirts and tights, baggy clothes, tight clothes, and lots of metal accessories. The style of dress crosses gender lines often, where males will wear eyeliner and even other makeup such as dark lipstick or eye shadow. Some makeup styles are creative for both male and female involving designs on the face. Many Goths also have tattoos. Some males will wear a kind of male skirt, usually as long as pants, with many buckles and straps on it. Since Goths stress individuality, they don't see solid lines between male and female clothing as we have been trained to by our culture. It is more about expressing yourself in your personal way.

The Goth philosophy and way of thinking does not really flow along religious lines. Many Goths are wiccan and pagan, but many are also from every one of the mainstream religions, including Christianity, of course. Since Goths value individuality, they don't have a set religion you must subscribe to. Many of the interests, as I mentioned, involve death and the dark side of life. However, this does *not* mean Goths like killing people or that they rejoice in murder. It is more of an expression and an acknowledgement that we all have a dark side of our personality, and death is a reality. Most Goths are intellectuals and detest violence. Most of the interest in the dark side of life is limited to literature and other entertainment, like horror movies. Going along with the horror interest is the affinity for vampires, bats, ghouls, and things of that nature. It is a myth that Goths want to be vampires or think they are vampires. There are always a few on the fringes of every culture that are a bit extreme, and those extreme people do not represent the main part of the culture. Thinking all Goths want to be vampires and suck blood is like thinking that every Christian is exactly like a televangelist.

Goths like music, literature, and style. They tend to be intellectual and perhaps more quiet than the average person. They share common interests and spend time together enjoying them. They may not smile much, but that does not mean they are evil or bad people. They merely see that there is a sad part of life, and acknowledge it.

Being a Christian Goth

As with any culture, even the mainstream ones, there are parts that are not compatible with Christianity. We all have to give up certain things to be Christians. A Goth can get too immersed in the culture and the sadness as a Christian. However, there is nothing in particular about being a Goth that keeps someone from being a Christian. In this case, I can speak from experience as I myself am a Goth. I am kind of a punk Goth, with interests from both cultures. One might think that a culture fascinated with darkness and death would not work well with Christianity. I have seen, however, that Christian Goths that know Jesus use their culture to point to Christ. We all are told we must die to ourselves as Christians. Die to our sin and our old way of living. Christian Goths also are aware of the suffering in our world that will be here until Jesus comes, and many of us mourn in our own way for that. So the black can be seen as a mourning for this world, and a representation of our death to self. Of course, as we have seen in this book, outward appearance and simple things like musical taste and style have very little to do with whether someone is a Christian or not. Yes, there are probably some types of music or literature that a Christian Goth should avoid, *just like every other Christian.* So a Christian Goth would keep the things from the Goth culture that did not interfere with his or her relationship with God. For each person, this may include different things. As long as God is kept first, then a Christian Goth, I believe, can be who they are.

I would like to recommend to you, if you are more interested in the Christian Goth movement, to check out the following web sites.

Christian Goth : www.christiangoth.com
Gothic Christianity: www.gothicchristianity.com

I also used the wikipedia entry for Goth as a source for this appendix, at:

http://en.wikipedia.org/wiki/Goth

Appendix B: Who are the Punks?

The punk culture began in the 1970's. Many punks say that the original punk movement is dead, because it has changed so much. The music, punk rock, or just punk, is very central to the punk culture. It is usually characterized by being edgy, simple, with shouted lyrics and heavy drums. Just like Goths, punks have many sub-types as well. Anarcho-punks, Crust-punk, hardcore, and skate punk (skaters) are a few.

Unlike Goths, punks are largely centered around their ideology. One of the main tenets of punk is a belief in personal freedom, to be able to do whatever you choose. This often is taken a bit further to a support of anarchy, basically a lack of government to tell people what to do. Being individual is very key to being a punk, and "selling out" by following the government or any institution is frowned upon. Punks also have a unique style of dress, usually to express that they are different from the mainstream. Spiked, colored hair and mohawks are popular. Also, ripped up clothing and metal spikes are worn. Since Goth and emo both come from punk, you may also see crossovers within these styles as well.

Since punk culture advocates freedom and dislikes government authority, a lot of it does focus on breaking the law as a form of protesting the control of government. However, many punks have grown past this type of thinking and while they still detest government control, they also dislike violence and drugs – things that have been associated with the punk movement.

Being a Christian Punk

There is an active Christian punk movement out there. In fact, it began in the 1980's as a response to the anti-religious aspect of punk. In some ways, being a punk Christian is about challenging the standard image of what it is to be a Christian. Much like the purpose of this book. Since punks do not like conformity and value individual thought, a Christian punk would not be as easily taken in by a lot of the legalism that can happen in the American church. Any Christian will have to give up parts of their culture that conflict with their faith, and a Christian punk is no exception. A Christian punk can still value individuality and freedom, while submitting to God and Jesus Christ as their lord. It is a simple matter of putting God ahead of any other beliefs. I believe that we can learn much from Christian punks, by realizing that many things we do to "conform" to the Christian church may not even be the right things to do. The Christian punks can help us see how we are narrowing the definition of how to be a Christian, and will help us have our freedom we have been given in Christ to be unique.

A Christian punk site I found that might interest you is:
http://www.christianpunks.co.uk/

I used the wikipedia article on punk as a source for this appendix.

http://en.wikipedia.org/wiki/Punk_subculture

Appendix C: Who are the fans?

There are fans of many things, but there are a certain type of fans that go to sci-fi, anime, and fantasy conventions. These fans are very much into a culture that some might classify as nerdy. They get together and play role playing games, or even live action role playing games where one dresses up as a character in a game. Some also love historical settings and go to renaissance faires or join the Society for Creative Anachronism (SCA), which celebrates and re-enacts medieval and renaissance times. Most of these people love great and fantastical stories. Literature, television, and movies are common interests. Things like the Stargate movies and series, the Lord of the Rings novels and movies, and Japanese animation (anime) shows bring them together.

Many of these fans love their interests so much they will write stories, create art, and even make costumes from these different settings. They will wear T-shirts and buy accessories like bags and purses with the logos of their favorite show on them. Perhaps you might think this unusual, but surely you have seen sports fans do the same kind of things. Some even paint their faces and wear crazy wigs to go to a game. These are simply fans of a different type.

Imagine a hotel with over 20,000 people gathered around a common interest of sci-fi, fantasy, and gaming. This would be a convention, and they happen all over the country, and in fact, around the world. Some have more specific themes, and are just sci-fi, or even just Star Trek. People gather together to talk about shared interests, meet famous actors, artists, and writers, play games, and share the costumes they have made.

Some of these people have trouble with Christians who think they are into the occult just because they like the fantasy stories about Harry Potter. Sometimes they are mocked just because they are out in public in a costume on a day *other* than Halloween. I am one of these people. We are nerds, geeks, otaku, gamers, cosplayers, rennies, SCAdians. Often outcast by mainstream society, we get together in our basements to play Dungeons and Dragons, or take a weekend to go to a convention together. We plan group costumes together from our favorite shows, and play Massively Multiplayer Online Roleplaying Games (MMORPGs) together over the internet.

Fans are of many different religions, and can be of any background. However, many of them are turned away from Christianity simply because something they do has been classified as evil. A lot of Christians think fantasy, anime, and roleplaying games are evil. For more on that, see the other appendices.

Being a Christian Fan

Being a Christian fan primarily involves making sure your fan interests do not become more important that your relationship with God. There is very little conflict between any of these interests and being a Christian. While some in the fan culture tend to be more liberal in values and lean toward pagan beliefs, that is not intrinsic to being a fan. As far as the books, shows, and movies, they are entertainment. Just as any Christian needs to filter out what entertainment they view, a Christian fan should as well. Some sci-fi shows and anime may not be something a Christian should watch. I will leave that up to the individual's conscience and relationship with God. Many young adults are fans of Harry Potter and Japanese anime and are afraid to tell their parents because many in the church think these things are evil by definition. This causes a rift in family relationships, and can cause children who grow up in Christian homes to want to leave the church when they get out on their own. Though it may not seem so unusual to have these interests, many fans do feel isolated, especially Christian fans. Once the church understands the nature of these fan interests correctly, I believe it will be more accepting of these people.

More information on Christian fandom can be found at:

www.fansforchrist.org

Appendix D: Christians watching Japanese Animation (Anime)

Simply put, Anime is animated film in the characteristic Japanese style. It can be compared to what we consider regular movies in the west.
The Wikipedia online encyclopedia has a good synopsis of anime:

> "Anime features a wide variety of genres and unique artistic styles which varies from artist to artist. It can have as many genres as live action cinema, including adventure, science fiction, children's stories, romance, medieval fantasy, erotica (hentai), occult/horror, action. Most anime includes a variety of thematic elements. For example, it is not uncommon for strongly action-themed anime to involve humor, romance, and even poignant social commentary, and romance-themed anime may involve a strong action element.
> Anime is often an explicitly commercial art form; producers and marketers aim for very specific audiences, with focused categories for shōnen (boys) and shōjo (girls) genres, as well as for teenagers and adults.".

Anime can be examined just like American movies

Just like in the American film industry, there are many ratings to Anime. It is best to refrain from assuming that it is all going to be G rated, and for children. There are certainly movies out there that some parents would not want their children to see, rated anywhere from G to NC-17. Anime is not so different. It has many genres, and many content levels. Just like with Hollywood films, the best advice is simply to be knowledgeable about the anime involved. Some anime is for mature audiences, yet this does not make all anime bad! There are plenty of anime titles that are romance, adventure, comedy, etc. just like regular movies that are perfectly acceptable for young viewers and Christian viewers.

Parent's Guide to Anime

The Anime café online has developed the Parent's Guide to
Anime, at

http://www.abcb.com/parents/

It gives general ratings of G, PG, and M to anime series and
movies. The PG list in my opinion is a good list of anime that I
would allow teens to watch. Some of the M series are similar to an
R rating. For instance, one of the best anime series ever, Cowboy
Bebop is listed there. It would be M because of the violence in it
mostly, plus occasional very brief nudity.

Anime and culture

A few generations ago, anime was just beginning to break into
American culture. Mostly this was as children's shows such as
Speed Racer and Astro Boy. Eventually, more adult shows made it
over, like Macross which was imported as Robotech. This was
marketed toward older children and early teens. Today, we have
many shows that originated in Japan on television. Anime is the
dominant form of media entertainment in Japan. It is not
considered to be for 'children' only. Whether it be children's
shows, cop dramas, soap operas, educational media, or otherwise,
it is still done in the animated style. Anime is used in schools as
well, as educational videos and in learning programs. To bulk it all
together as either 'Childish' OR 'Violent and Mature' would be
impossible. Many anime shows have a greater depth of story,
character, and development that American 'cartoons'. Some are
sheerly entertainment, and some are greatly thought provoking.
The younger generation is finding anime as a fun alternative to
kid's cartoons, while much anime on TV has strong appeal for
teens as it combines the fun of quality animation but addresses
more mature themes of romance and real life. Many adults watch
anime as well; there are many titles with the maturity and depth of
story for adults to find them entertaining.

Christians watching Anime

When it comes down to it, anime is just like any other form of entertainment. Each Christian will have to judge what he can and cannot watch as part of a relationship with God. Some have fantasy themes with magic as part of the world, which will be addressed in the Appendix E, Christians, Fantasy and Magic. The next time you meet someone who watches anime, ask them about the shows they watch and you will learn more about the diversity of stories that are found in this genre.

A good place to learn about Christianity and anime is:

www.christiananime.net

The wikipedia entry on anime was used as a source for this appendix:

http://en.wikipedia.org/wiki/Anime

Appendix E: Christians, Fantasy, and Magic

Many Christians, young and old, enjoy great stories of literature. Many of these stories have good moral lessons in them, and many inspire us to be more than what they are. Some of these stories include references to magic. Many of these tales are set in what we call a "fantasy" setting. Typical fantasy settings include mythical creatures such as dragons and unicorns, and have people in them, good and evil, that use magic.

The key here for a Christian, and I think most Christians are aware of this, is that the term is "fantasy." Most stories, including the oft debated Harry Potter, are set in fantasy worlds. Just in case you aren't clear on what this means, let's take a look at the word fantasy on dictionary.com.

Fantasy

1.   imagination, esp. when extravagant and unrestrained.
2.   the forming of mental images, esp. wondrous or strange fancies; imaginative conceptualizing.

Fantasy primarily involves the imagination. These are imaginary worlds. In essence, they are not real. Most people that are in their right state of mind that read these books and love the stories and movies of fantasy know that it is not about real life. In fact, that is why they like it. It is a beautiful tale of an imaginary place, perhaps a struggle, and a hero that most often fights for what is good. People can forget about the rent being due and the lousy weather and the oil having to be changed on the car. For a while, at least.

Real Magic and Fantasy Magic

The "magic" we are forbidden to practice in the Bible comes from Satan. Pure and simple. That is why we are forbidden to be involved in it. However, in almost every fantasy novel, Satan doesn't even exist in the universe. It is a different reality, a different universe. The magic there is not the "magic" of this real world. Magic, in these stories, is more like a natural force that is used. You could compare it to gravity, or electricity in the real world. And people that read these stories know this. We are not deluded into thinking somehow we can make a magic wand and cast spells and fly around. We know better. In fact, as Christians, we should know that idols and made up things have no power.

> We know that an idol is nothing at all in the world and that there is no God but one. -- 1 Corinthians 8:4

We know that an **idol is nothing.** It doesn't have any power. Neither does anything made up from the fantasy world, because it is not real. Just as an idol is a god someone made up that does not really exist. As Christians, we should have no fear of anything made up. We serve the real God, the *only* God.

Imagination is a gift

God gave us all imagination. We are to live in the real world, yes, but without imagination there is no creativity. There is no art without imagination, no music. These things exist first in the mind before they are brought forth. Stories about fantasy places are part of the gift of imagination. What makes us unique as humans is our ability to create and see things in our mind that do not exist. Exercising the imagination grows our ability to create new things.

One of our greatest Christian authors wrote fantasy novels: C.S. Lewis. He loved Greek mythology and other fantastic tales. He wrote the Chronicles of Narnia; a series of fantasy stories that point toward Christ. However he also wrote *Mere Christianity,* one of the greatest Christian literary works defending faith in Christ. His gift through story allowed many young readers to learn about Christ through the lion, Aslan, who also dies to save his friends. Many people, Christian and not, love the Narnia books. Many people, through C.S. Lewis, have developed an interest in Christianity, have even come to Christ, I dare say – and some of that is because of his fantasy books. Yes, there is magic in those books, and not all of it is evil. It is simply a force, as I mentioned, in that other, unreal world. C.S. Lewis used his imagination to give us a beautiful story about Christ, his love, his death, and his resurrection – through fantasy.

Not Judging Others

If the topic of magic disturbs you or makes you uncomfortable, you are free to not read fantasy novels or watch those movies. However, it does not mean it is wrong for every Christian. It was what I would call a Romans 14 issue, as I talk about in Chapter 6 of this book. Some things, like reading about magic, do not interfere with a Christian's relationship with God. Perhaps it does for some, but not for all. Each person should be sincere before God in what they do.

If we continue to tell people who read Harry Potter and who like movies like Lord of the Rings that they are in the occult, worshipping the devil, or going to hell, we will simply continue to keep those people away from Christ and Christians. Not to mention the fact that this is simply wrong.

The Real Occult

There are those who practice the actual occult. What they do is nothing like what is talked about in fantasy novels. If it was anything like that, we would see people flying, creating fire from their hands, and teleporting on a regular basis. Perhaps once in a very great while some powerful occult event might happen, but certainly this is not what the daily life of say, a real world magician or devil worshipper is like. People who try to practice real magic want *power*. People who read fantasy novels want *entertainment*. There is a huge difference.

Most real occultists would laugh at you if you suggested that reading Harry Potter was a way to learn "real magic." It would almost be insulting to them. Christians who don't understand the difference often associate the two together, yet the reality is much different. Of course I am not going into detail here on how to practice the occult, but I will tell you it does not involve magic wands and eye of newt.

Words of Caution

As with any interest, fantasy can interfere with a Christian's life if it is taken too seriously. If someone is involved too much in the fantasy world and not enough in reality, the fantasy itself is not the problem – it is a symptom. Something in that person's life is driving them away from wanting to be in the real world. Whatever that is, it is what should be dealt with. When I was a teenager for a while I was depressed about my parents' divorce and I spent most of my time playing fantasy games and reading fantasy novels. It was an escape for me. Does this mean fantasy is bad? No, but being in fantasy too much of course is. I stopped caring about school and my grades. Not because the fantasy was so wonderful, but because I was depressed about the divorce.

The problem I had to deal with was accepting the divorce and getting on with my life. Did I have to throw away my fantasy novels and games to do that? No. Today I still enjoy reading fantasy and watching the movies that come out, including the ones based on J.R.R. Tolkein's *The Lord of the Rings.* He was a Christian author as well, and his stories include a positive aspect and a reverence for life and what is good.

Live in reality, enjoy your imagination

Regardless of whether you like fantasy, it is just that: imaginary. Not real. We all can live in the real world with Christ, yet enjoy using the imagination he has given us. Children love stories about talking animals and other fantasy, should we take all that away from them out of an overreaction? I loved dreaming about knights and dragons as a child, and it brought me happiness. Still, inside, we are all children; God's children. To him, we will always be childlike. It is beautiful and wonderful to imagine; it is a gift from God. Our imagination brings out the creative side in all of us and leads to beautiful art and music. Let us not stifle it in our legalism. An idol is nothing, and magic from an imaginary world doesn't hurt anyone. It is simply a way to express and enjoy what we have. As we live our lives in Christ, let us never forget the childlike wonder of the imagination he has given us.

Appendix F: Christians Playing Dungeons and Dragons

Dungeons and Dragons has long been described by certain
Christians as a 'doorway to occultism' and a 'manual for magic.' I
will first address what D&D is. This will include describing a
typical game session, including examples of games I have been in.
Then I will address specific claims and charges about the game,
which I believe are patently false.

What is Dungeons and Dragons?

Dungeons and Dragons (or D&D) originated from an already
existing game of medieval warfare. This game, Chainmail, was
further developed into the first true *role-playing game.* (Wikipedia,
1) A role playing game is where the player takes on the role of
someone else, and acts out that role. This may seem a bit strange at
first, but people actually do this for a living; they are called actors.
So, this game gave people a chance to become actors, playing a
part.

   The director of this movie, if you will, was known as the
Dungeon Master. This person was sort of the referee who created
the world and the other characters that the players would interact
with in their own movie. (Now this person is usually called the
Game Master, since role-playing games have evolved to have
many settings beyond fantasy.)

   The genre, or setting of this game is fantasy. It is very
similar to the world of Middle-Earth in J.R.R. Tolkein's *Lord of
the Rings* novels. The general fantasy world is the world of wizards
and knights, fair maidens and dragons, elves, dwarves, goblins,
trolls, kings and peasants. Of course, this world in some ways is
similar to our medieval and renaissance times, in terms of
government, clothing, weapons and armor.

   So, a player of D&D creates this persona, the role they
would play, which is known as their *character*. A character in
D&D has ability scores that describe how strong, smart, fast, and
charming they are, for instance. They also have a sex, height, race
(such as elf, dwarf, or human) and a *class*, which is their job. The
current version of D&D, 3.5, allows many choices for this class. A
character is some type of adventurer (obviously, you'd get bored

playing as a peasant farming all day or scrubbing in the kitchens.) The classes a player can choose for their character are based loosely on different fantasy stereotypes you have probably seen in movies. Here are a few examples: warrior, barbarian, wizard, rogue, priest, ranger (a woodsman or hunter), paladin (like a knight), monk (think Kung Fu.)

Usually, characters are part of a group of adventurers whose strengths compliment each other. This group is referred to as a *party*. If you have seen Lord of the Rings, think of how Gandalf can use magic, Aragorn can use swords, Boromir can fight and shoot the bow, and the hobbits are good at hiding and sneaking around. In different situations, different party members' abilities are needed. This actually promotes a sense of teamwork within the group of adventurers.

Playing the Game

Once the characters have been created, it is time to play. The Game Master will usually start the adventurers on a long-term quest usually referred to as a *campaign*. The characters meet in the fantasy world, join together and begin on their quest.

There are many rules that determine what a character can and cannot do. They are based on the abilities mentioned before, such as strength, and also skills that the character learns. As a character gains experience in the game, *experience points* are awarded. This is a way for characters to advance their skills. As they gain experience, skills and abilities improve.

The game in some ways tries to simulate what it would be like if your character was actually there in the fantasy world. Let's compare this to a task you would perform. You have a bow and arrow, and you are fairly skilled with it. So, you go practice at the archery range shooting at the targets. Now, even though you are good, do you hit the bull's-eye *every* time? No. Sometimes you do, and sometimes you don't. Sometimes you don't even know why you missed. However, if you had no skill with the bow, you would probably never hit the bull's-eye, or, if you did, it would be total luck. To represent this situation in D&D, your skill is added to a random dice roll. Here is an example of how this would work. This time, it is your character Visk that is skilled with the bow. To represent this skill, he gets a skill score of 8. (Zero would be no skill at all and 20 would be the best possible.) To represent random chance each time you fire, a dice roll is added to your score. Hitting the bull's-eye is represented by a difficulty of 15. So, each time you roll your dice, you add your score of 8. If the total is **15 or above**, your character hit the bull's-eye. So, this sequence describes the action rolling a 20-sided die (results of 1-20):

Roll	+Score	=Total	Result
11	+8	=19	Visk hit the bullseye
6	+8	=14	Visk just missed the bullseye
20	+8	=28	A perfect shot
2	+8	=10	Visk missed badly

The player would roll the die (die being singular for dice), and the Game Master would tell you the result of the action. This is how many actions occur in D&D. Other actions, such as getting on a horse or picking up a rock on the ground, are simple and do not require a dice roll. It is assumed that you are able to do it. To do something like this, a player just says, "I get on my horse." So now the rest of the gamers all know that that player is on his horse.

An Example Gaming Session

As luck would have it, I played in a D&D game just a week ago. There were seven of us who went out to a gaming café. We sat around a table and got comfy on the couches. A TV was playing in the background and *Rocky II* was on, though I don't know why.

Many people assume that when gamers role-play they totally take on the character. Usually, this is not what happens at all. In fact I have never seen this happen, and if I did, I would think that the person doing it was a total nutcase. Instead, we all have a picture of our character in our minds, doing the things we are trying to do with him or her. Besides that, its not much different than friends gathering around to play monopoly or cards. We talk, laugh, joke, and play the game. During this session, for example, we took a break and walked next door to get pizza and subs. Let me give you an example dialogue from this game.* The players are

Scribe, Adryn, Steve (myself), Brad, John, and Lex. The Game
Master is Dan.

Dan: Okay, so last time you guys played you had just killed all the
wolves that the warrior guy had sent after you.
Steve: Yeah, I had just climbed up to the platform and then
collapsed there bleeding. So I'm up there. Bleeding.
John: Okay I go look back to the room the wolves came from,
behind the gate.
Dan: What gate?
John: The one to the room with the wolves.
Dan: Oh, that gate rose up into the ceiling, there's just an empty
room where the wolves were.
John: Oh ok.
Scribe: Oh, this is such a bad movie.
Steve: What? Rocky II is a great movie! Its like… nostalgia.
Scribe: No it's not, it's just bad.
Brad: See I think watching movies is like a meal, sometimes you
want something really healthy, but sometimes you want some junk
food. So movies like this are just junk food.
Adryn: Yeah, I can see that.
Steve: THIS IS A GOOD MOVIE!
John: So anyway, I guess we all climb up to the platform.
Steve: Yeah, is anyone going to heal me?
John: Okay, let me see. I have one Cure Light Wounds spell left.
Steve: Well? Heal me!
John: Okay, I cast the spell. (John rolls some dice.)You heal seven
hit points.
Steve: Okay, thanks. Now I'm up to 10.
Dan: Alright, what are you guys going to do now that you all
climbed up to the platform?
Steve: Well I guess I will scout ahead. I signal to the rest of the
party to be quiet and wait where they are.
Scribe: WHAT? YOU WANT US TO WAIT?
Steve: So much for stealth.
Dan: Okay you see a door on the right and a room over to the left.
Steve: Okay I go into the room.
Dan: This room right here, you just walk in?
Steve: Okay no wait, I check for traps first.

Dan: Alright give me a roll.

Steve: (Rolls dice) Total is 31.

Dan: Yeah, you find a trip wire going across the floor here.

Scribe: I walk up behind the rogue.

Steve: What are you doing? I told you guys to stay back! There's a trap here.

Scribe: Well, get rid of it, rogue!

Steve: What do you think I'm doing? Okay Dan, I get out my grappling hook and move back away from the trap and have everyone else back up. (Meaningful look at Scribe)

Dan: Okay. (He moves our miniatures on the map to show where we moved to.)

Steve: Alright I throw the grappling hook across the wire and use it to pull the tripwire.

Dan: Ok roll. (Steve rolls dice) You hear a loud *thunk*.

Steve: Okay I go carefully check what happened.

Adryn: Wow Billy Dee Williams sure looks different in this movie.

John: Yeah but you can still tell that's his voice when he talks.

Steve: What? That's not Billy Dee Williams.

John: Remember in Star Wars he was the only guy who called Han "Han", everyone else said it like "Hahn."

Scribe: Yeah, that's right.

Steve: That is *so* not Billy Dee Williams… its… its some other guy.

Lex: I think he is right.

John: No way that is totally him.

Steve: No its this other guy who went on to make this other movie… its Carl Weathers, that's it. Carl Weathers.

Scribe: I'll settle this. (Gets out her cell phone and calls someone.)

Dan: Okay well you see a bunch of metal spears that are stuck in the wall now.

Steve: Wow glad I found that trap.

Brad: I walk by and look at the spears. Hmm.

Scribe: (on phone) Okay you know that Rocky movie? Yeah. Who plays that guy... (*pause*) Apollo Creed.

Steve: No, that's the *character's* name not the actor!

Scribe: Oh. (pause) It's Carl Weathers.

Steve: Ha! I told you.

John: Okay but he still really looks like Billy Dee Williams.

*This is from memory and not exact.

As you can see, this is hardly an occult experience we were having. Instead, it is like a bunch of friends getting together playing a game. I have played D&D for almost 20 years, and this experience is very typical. I have played with probably a dozen different groups of people, and it all has been very much like this.

Defending the Game

The chief complaint I see about D&D by certain Christians is the magic. Specifically, that somehow D&D either teaches real magic use, or is a front for people to lure the unsuspecting into the occult. An article on the Chick web site (maker of extreme Christian tracts) references many of these arguments, and somehow claims to have researched these things. However, in many cases, no example is given from D&D as to how these things are the case. I will use <u>this article</u> as a source later in this section. If you read the D&D sourcebooks, it is clear it is a game. The rulebooks are just that; a collection of rules to describe how to play the game. It seems that if some of the critics actually read the books, they would see there is no way to actually perform any "real magic" from them. Otherwise, wouldn't we have hordes of teenagers out there purchasing these books and hurling *fireballs* and *magic missiles* at each other? To defend D&D and show it does not conflict with Christianity, I will examine the criticisms of this article. I will also show examples from the D&D books themselves. To prepare for this section, I just have read the entire section on Magic in the 3rd edition rulebooks. I will also examine some other criticisms of the game and explain why they are flawed.

Morality

One of the claims that is made often is that the players (often portrayed as young, impressionable teens, though this is hardly the norm) are offered confusing choices on morality. For instance, in the game, your character has an *alignment*. This alignment determines your characters general moral stance. The purpose of alignment in the game, as quoted by the Player's Handbook is "a tool for developing your character's identity...Each alignment represents a broad range of personality types or personal philosophies." In real life, there are good and bad people. In movies there are good and bad people. So, why not in a game? Critics often say that because there is evil in the game, it encourages people to be evil in real life. This is like saying that watching Star Wars might make you decide to become like Darth Vader.

In every epic story or movie, there is always evil to overcome. *Someone* has to play the bad guy. Your character's morality helps you know more about him or her. So, you can decide what they would do in certain situations. Using Star Wars again, Han Solo was a "good" character, but not *that* good. Remember Luke had to talk him into rescuing the princess by offering him a lot of money.

Luke: "But they're going to kill her."
Han: "Better her than me."
Luke: "She is rich."
Han: "Rich?"
Luke: "Yes. Rich. Powerful. Listen, if you were to rescue her, the reward would be..."
Han: "What?"
Luke: "Well more wealth, than you can imagine."
Han: "I can imagine quite a bit."
Luke: "You'll get it."
Han: "I better."

Han might well be described as having the alignment of Chaotic Good, which is described as:

"A chaotic good character acts as his conscience directs him with little regard for what others expect of him. He makes his own way, but he is kind and benevolent. He...has little use for laws and regulations... He follows his own moral compass, which, although good, may not agree with society..." (Players Handbook, 89)

So, alignment is simply background for your character. A criticism leveled at D&D comes from a description of the Lawful Evil alignment. This is from Schnoebelen's article from the Chick site:

> "For example, you can have a "lawful evil" character. A handbook states that: "A lawful evil villain methodically takes what he wants within the limits of his code of conduct without regard to whom it hurts. He cares about tradition, loyalty and order, but not about freedom, dignity or life." Talk about a mish-mash of moral ambiguity. Our young people are having enough trouble getting their values straight without being immersed in this sort of material!" (Schnoebelen)

Yet, there are plenty of characters in the Bible who fit this description. I would say Pharaoh in Exodus is a good example. He took what he wanted with little regard for others, by enslaving the Jews. He had his order and tradition, but did not value freedom or dignity of life. Admitting that there are people like this is hardly a corruption of one's values.

Fantasy Magic is not Real World Magic

The magic that we are forbidden to practice in the Bible comes from one source – Satan. God and Satan are here in the *real* world with us. Fantasy stories take place in *other* worlds, in other realities that never have happened and never will. It is important to note that in many fantasy worlds, like D&D, magic is *different* than what we might call 'magic' in the real world we live in. Magic in these fantasy worlds is considered a natural force. I would compare it to something like electricity or even gravity. Using magic in these worlds is like turning on a lamp or making furniture. It is simply there, part of the lives of the characters that live in the imaginary fantasy world. It is *not* the occult magic that is referred to in the world of reality. When a character in the fantasy world accesses magic, they are simply tapping into a power source that is built into their world, *not* calling on evil spirits, demons, or the devil.

If a game is supposed to be set in a fantasy world, it is hardly surprising that it might include magic in that world. It wouldn't be very exciting to play a game called "Checkbooks and Yard Work" that was totally based in reality would it? Magic adds an element for our imagination to enjoy when we are stuck mowing the lawn. It's simply imagination. To say D&D is bad purely for including magic would be to categorize *any* story that includes some type of magic as evil. We would then have to classify Cinderella, the Smurfs, Lord of the Rings, Mario Brothers, and a whole horde of stories and ideas as evil and corruptive. This would include the famous *Chronicles of Narnia* by C.S. Lewis, the oft-quoted Christian writer.

D&D and arcane rituals

Often critics will claim that somehow D&D contains information on how to 'really' cast spells and perform magical rituals. The first page of the introduction in the Players Handbook clearly states, "This game is fantasy. The action of a D&D game takes place in the imaginations of the players…In reality, however, you are no more your player than you are the king when you play chess. Likewise, the world implied by these rules is an imaginary one." (Players Handbook, 6) In his article, Straight Talk on Dungeons and Dragons, William Schnoebelen (who says he was a former "witch") asserts:

> "On top of that, the second issue is that the materials themselves, in many cases, contain authentic magical rituals… In the late 1970's, a couple of the game writers actually came to my wife and I as prominent "sorcerers" in the community. **They wanted to make certain the rituals were authentic.** For the most part, they are." (Schnoebelen)

This is one of the most profoundly undocumented claims this writer makes. It is completely off base. Why, you ask? Because, there is *no* description of any ritual in the D&D core rulebooks. If the author wanted to make this point he should have provided an example. But there aren't any. Now, in the 70's there was Basic D&D and Advanced D&D. (D&D History) I owned original books for these versions. There are no details on rituals to perform in these books, from what I can remember. As I said, I just completed reading the entire magic section of my current rulebooks just to make certain this is the case with the new books. What is in there is very simply *rules*, and not ritual. This is a description of casting a spell from the Player's Handbook:

"Preparing a spell requires careful reading from a spellbook (for wizards) or devout prayers or mediation (for divine spellcasters)... after preparing a spell, *the character* carries it, nearly cast, in his or her mind, ready for use...Spellcasting might require a few special words, specific gestures, a specific item, or any combination of the three." (Players Handbook, 148, emphasis added)

Note that is the character, not the player, that is actually performing these actions. The player does not have a spellbook, nor does he meditate. It is just assumed the character does something to this effect, but it is not explicitly described. The player looks up the exact spell they want in the rulebook so they can understand the effects in the game. I'll show you an example of one of the most common spells, Fireball.

Fireball
Level: Sor/Wiz 3
Components: V,S,M
Casting Time: 1 action
Range: Long (400 ft. + 40 ft./level)
Area: 20-ft radius spread
Duration: Instantaneous
Saving throw: Reflex half
Spell Resistance: Yes

A *fireball* spell is a burst of flame that detonates with a low roar and deals 1d6 points of fire damage per caster level (maximum 10d6) to all creatures within the area. Unattended objects also take this damage…

You point your finger and determine the range (distance and height) at which the fireball is to burst. A glowing pea-sized bead streaks from the pointing digit and, unless it impacts upon a material body or solid barrier prior to attainting the prescribed range, blossoms into the fireball at that point… (Players Handbook, 204)

There is a bit more describing the effects such as things catching on fire, etc. However, there is nothing in the description of this spell or *any other* spell in the D&D manuals that will instruct you how to cast it for "real". I suppose you could try pointing your finger and hoping a "glowing pea-sized bead" streaks out; good luck with that. The components section lists "**V,S,M**" meaning to cast the spell your character has to say a **V**erbal part (some magic words), a **S**omatic part (waving the hands and gesturing) and also a **M**aterial part, which in this case is a ball of bat guano (eww) and sulfur. There is no description for *any* of these spells saying exactly what the verbal and somatic parts are. Therefore it does not tell you how to cast the spell. Not that anyone can really cast a fireball spell anyway (if you have seen someone do this, feel free to correct me.)

The absurdity of the claim that D&D manuals can help you cast spells is illustrated in a wonderful article entitled "Spellcasting 101" by William J Watson. He tries to cast the spell *Hold Portal* from the 3rd edition books:

…the spell description says that "the magic holds the portal fast, just as if it were securely closed and normally locked." That should easily keep my two daughters from running out of the playroom every two minutes to bother me as I write this.

Test Method: The book tells me that the only thing we need to cast this spell is a verbal component... **but it doesn't tell me what that magic word is.** Still, a 20th level mage like myself should know all of this by now. I'll just shout a few lock-related *magical power words* at the playroom door.

Results: Failure.

(<u>Watson</u>, emphasis added.)

I highly recommend this article to illustrate the point. The fact is that players do not even say any magic words or move their hands or do any kind of ritual *whatsoever*. The words and gestures are left to the imagination, and the player simply says, "I cast Fireball." That is it. No rituals, no magic words, no eye of newt. Just, "I cast Fireball" with maybe an "at those guys over there" after it.

Violence in the Game

One thing that has to be kept in mind is that D&D did come from a war game. A large part of it is based on medieval warfare. A good movie example of this kind of thing is *Braveheart,* with Mel Gibson. People really fought with swords and lances and shields and it was brutal. In the game, you can fight as well. Personally, one of the things I like about the game is you can fight monsters. In real life, really the only fight that could be challenging is against a human opponent. Killing people is clearly wrong but killing an evil, nasty, slimy monster with 16 eyeballs in a fantasy game is great fun. However, you have a choice, and actions have consequences just like in real life. If you take your party and slaughter a village of innocents, word will get around about what you did and good characters will come after you. In fact, I have often found D&D contains lessons in morality. If you play an evil character, you eventually make enemies. You lie and betray others. People stop trusting you. Others are after you. You often die alone and friendless. Evil reaps its rewards just as it does in real life, while good characters make friends, save lives and help others. They end up with allies and victories. Though they may make evil enemies in the process, they are trusted and known as a good hero.

I want to point out that fighting and casting spells are by no means the only things players do. Players role-play. As their character they discuss options, talk to townspeople, solve puzzles, scout the landscape, create items, and many other things. Fighting is only a part of the big story that is played out as your character goes through an adventure. Sometimes a character can even talk his way out of fighting. It all depends on the player's choices.

In terms of violence, it is really dependent on the players. Combat is handled through *hit points,* which represent the amount of hits a character can take. Many gamers simply do combat by talking hit points. For instance, "Okay, I hit it with my sword for 10 points of damage." No gory details needed. It is a game and when you are fighting the point is to survive and defeat the enemy, so you are essentially trying to get the enemy down to zero hit points while keeping yours above zero. It's really a game of numbers. The numbers help describe who wins and loses. Some players and game masters can be more descriptive by saying for instance, "you slash the orc across the torso for 5 points of damage." This is no more violent, however, than your typical action movie.

D&D and negative psychological effects

Another frequent criticism of this game is that it causes violence, suicide, or some type of disorder where the player loses a sense of reality. Several studies have been done testing this hypothesis, and ***none of them found a link between these and Dungeons and Dragons.*** An article I found from **religioustolerance.org** lists five separate studies, and none of them found links to D&D. In fact, one study found that the suicide rate among role-players is over 50 times less than the average population. Another found that gamers are less likely to commit crimes. (Robinson, 3)

What about the cases where this *has* happened? There are often stories you hear about D&D players losing it and thinking the game is reality, or that D&D was involved in a crime. However, many of these stories are simply urban legends, or police ended up determining that D&D had nothing to do with the crime. (Wikipedia) Of course there are a few cases where this did happen. Since we have already established that D&D does not cause these problems, it is logical to assume the people in these cases had prior mental disorders. The tiny number of actual cases where gamers are involved in crimes, again, shows that they are less likely to exhibit violent behavior than the average person.

What about the demons in D&D?

One thing that is helpful to understand about D&D is that it takes concepts that it considers to be from various mythologies to build a fantasy world. The game master can use these concepts to create various fantasy flavors. For instance, it could be Norse, Egyptian, Oriental, Celtic, or even Native American in style. The creatures that a player can encounter come from almost every one of these possible mythologies. Christianity is not the only religion to talk about "demons." For instance, Japanese mythology has a type of demon called an *Oni*.

> **Oni** are devil-like demons with long nails, wild hair, a fierce look and two horns on their forehead like the devil images known in Western Christian cultures. They wear tiger skins and can fly. Oni hunt for the souls of those who did evil things in their lives. (Japanese Mythology)

In fact, since demons are not really given a physical description in the Bible, it may be Christianity was influenced by demon concepts from other cultures. The point is that the "demons" in D&D are not directly correlated with the Christian concept of demons.

The truth is, in the 20 years I have played D&D, I have had my characters encounter demons maybe twice. There are such a wide variety of monsters and creatures in the game that demons rarely show up.

Back in 2nd edition D&D, TSR (the company that formerly owned D&D) actually removed all references to demons, in what was believed to be a gesture toward the religious pressure on it. However, they were placed back into 3rd edition by the new company, Wizards of the Coast. (Wikipedia)

Personally, as a Christian, I will say I don't like the idea that there are "demons" in D&D. I would rather there not be, and in any games that I run myself I exclude them. I know that demons are real and would rather not play around with the concept. Since D&D is so versatile, it should be no problem to fully enjoy D&D without including any demons.

I found out in my research that 3rd edition released a book just on demons and demon worshippers. It is called the *Book of Vile Darkness* and is for "Mature" readers only. This is not part of the core rules, and is definitely *not required* to play the game. In defense of the D&D publishers, I would say that they probably don't believe in demons and think of this as another "mythology" to add to the campaign. For example, in the movies *Young Sherlock Holmes* and *Indiana Jones and the Temple of Doom* the heroes were up against strange cults that worshipped evil gods and peformed human sacrifice.

Regardless, as a Christian, I would recommend for a good D&D experience just to cut out the demons altogether.

Sex and D&D

D&D is a fantasy world where characters can experience new adventures, conquer enemies, win rewards, gain experience and even find love. Since you are only limited by your imagination, your character could do just about anything, including have sex. However, this game is definitely not designed for this purpose. There are no sections or chapters on characters having sex.

Christians have certain guidelines to follow on sex, and they would apply to playing this game as well. Just as they apply to watching movies, or other types of entertainment. Therefore, a player should keep these guidelines when playing D&D.

Do the rulebooks feature some scantily clad women? Yes. This is part of the fantasy genre. If you go to the library and look in the fantasy section, there will be many of these. (I dare say the same about the romance novel section.) D&D is not marketed to Christians, obviously. There is no actual nudity beyond the occasional breast in the books I have seen, and those are the older rule books. I just paged through all 286 pages of the Players Handbook. I found only 3 pictures with scantily clad women, none of which appear sexually suggestive. They are either just standing there or casting a spell. I think this may be part of marketing also to attract more women players by having less of those types of drawings and artwork in the newer books.

Benefits of D&D

Dungeons and Dragons, as we have seen from an earlier description, actually requires math skills. It does not require advanced math, but it does require regular addition, subtraction and multiplication. Practicing these things in the context of a game actually encourages math development among the players.

The Swedish National Board for Youth Affairs published a report on role-playing, describing it as a stimulating hobby that promotes creativity. (Wikipedia) The National Association of Gifted-Creative Children has endorsed D&D for its educational content. (Robinson, 3) D&D does actively encourage creative problem solving. There are puzzles to solve, social situations to resolve, and decisions to be made about actions and consequences.

The Imagination

I find that one of the most beautiful parts of D&D is the chance to stretch the imagination. A player can imagine other worlds, mystical creatures, endless seas, magnificent cities and more. When we were children we imagined things like this, at least I would say most of us did. Isn't our imagination a gift from God? Where did the great painters get their ideas for paintings if they did not first see them in their mind's eye? The great building and structures of our time were first imagined in the mind of an architect. As adults we should be free to imagine and enjoy the gift we have. We imagine differently from children, this is true, but we still imagine. We played "cops and robbers" as kids, can't we play Dungeons and Dragons as adults? I say we can, and we can enjoy it.

Accepting Christians who play D&D

D&D is not for everyone. I'm not saying that Christians have to play D&D or even *like* D&D. However, Christians should, after learning the facts, be able to accept other Christians playing the game. In Romans 14 Paul writes:

> The man who eats everything must not look down on him who does not, and the man who does not eat everything must not condemn the man who does, for God has accepted him. Who are you to judge someone else's servant? To his own master he stands or falls.

Christians playing D&D are not sinning and not becoming involved in the occult. As this article has demonstrated:

- Role-playing involves imagination and fun, not a departure from reality
- The D&D sourcebooks are primarily a listing of rules to play a game, not instructions for the occult
- No credible link has been established between D&D and suicide, violence, or other mental disorders
- D&D does have some content that Christians should be wary of
- Playing D&D can have educational and creative benefits

Playing D&D as a Christian should be viewed as any other entertainment. Some movies and books we are ok to read, and some we should not. Just as we can eat too much cake or watch too much football, we can play too much D&D. As Christians this is how we function in the secular world. We can do many things, within reason and limits. If we have a peach with a bad part, do we throw the whole peach away? We can, or we can cut the small bad part out with a knife and eat the rest of the peach which is perfectly good. D&D is not just one game, it is really an almost limitless structure within which a player can have adventures. Christians can play easily within this structure without going astray.

Biblical Perspective

I would be remiss if I did not put this article in perspective of the Bible. Interestingly, in the article on the Chick web site, the author quotes I Thessalonians 5:22 as saying: "Abstain from all appearance of evil." This is from the King James Version. This appears to be a slightly inaccurate translation in the KJV, as three modern versions, the NIV, NASB, and New Living, translate it as such (respectively):

Avoid every kind of evil.

abstain from every form of evil.

Keep away from every kind of evil.

Paul the Apostle, and author of this book, was not talking about appearances at all, but evil itself. The author of the Chick article is apparently ignoring other versions of the Bible to make *his* point, which is actually about appearance. However, we know God does not judge things by appearance.

The LORD does not look at the things man looks at. Man looks at the outward appearance, but the LORD looks at the heart - 1 Samuel 16:7

Just because someone dresses differently from you, or looks like what your 'culture' might consider evil, does not mean they *are* evil. The next time you hear someone saying evil about D&D, tell them to look for themselves. Not at the appearance, but at the actual game and the people who play it.

Sources:

Spellcasting 101: Don't Try This At Home, William J. Walton
http://www.theescapist.com/random011102.htm

Should a Christian Play Dungeons & Dragons? William
Schnoebelen http://www.chick.com/articles/frpg.asp

Straight Talk on Dungeons and Dragons, William Schnoebelen
http://www.chick.com/articles/dnd.asp

Dungeons and Dragons, Players Handbook, 3rd Edition, Wizards of
the Coast

Wikipedia entry for Dungeons and Dragons:
http://en.wikipedia.org/wiki/Dungeons_&_Dragons

Dungeons & Dragons - history, versions, and revisions
http://www.lyberty.com/encyc/articles/d_and_d.html

Dungeons and Dragons™ and other fantasy role-playing games,
B.A. Robinson
http://www.religioustolerance.org/d_a_d.htm

Japanese Mythology
http://www.artelino.com/articles/japanese_mythology.asp

About the Author

Stephen Weese has been a Christian and a freak almost his entire life. He was saved at the age of ten and started playing Dungeons and Dragons when he was twelve. In elementary school he got a Commodore 64 which also turned him into a geek. As he was studying Computer Science in college, he became an assistant to a pastor at a small Baptist church where he began ministry training. He gave sermons at church and spoke at campus Christian groups while attending leadership conferences at a charismatic church. At that time he also began playing Live Action Role Playing (LARP) games. Stephen has been teaching computer classes at the college level for over eight years now and holds a Master's degree in Computer Information Technology. The book he co-wrote, the *A+ Exam Prep*, was the number one selling title for Coriolis Press. His ministry, Fans for Christ, a group for Christian fans of anime, sci-fi, role playing, goth, and other similar interests, has been around since 2003 and is online at *www.fansforchrist.org*. His hobbies include music and acting as well as auto racing. He lives in North Carolina has a pet lovebird named Freek.